# EVEREST IN MIND



Author
Sudheer Reddy Pamireddy

Translated By
Rachana Srungavarapu

**EVEREST IN MIND**

First Edition: May 2022
ISBN (Paperback) 978-81-956773-2-0
ISBN (E-Book) 978-81-956773-3-7



**Published By**
Kasturi Vijayam,
3-50, Main Road,
Dokiparru Village -521322
Krishna Dist., Andhra Pradesh, India.

**Author**
Sudheer Reddy Pamireddy

+91 95150 54998.
Email: kasturivijayam@gmail.com

**Dedicated to**

Though you had been on this earth and with us only for a short span of nine months, your memory will be with us forever as the sensitivity of a leaf in our hearts. We dedicate our thoughts, opinions, research, and experiences of our literary journey to **Chintapalli PurnaSri.**

Padmaja (Elder sister)
Sudheer Reddy Pamireddy (Brother-in-law)

# Acknowledgements

From the bottom of my heart, I thank my parents, Smt Satyavathi and Sri Pitchireddy Pamireddy. I must recognize my better half, Padmaja, who has been with me in all the times of difficulties and supported me all the way. I bless the sunlight of my life, my children, Kaushik Reddy Pamireddy and Tejo Samiksha, for giving their time and sharing valuable inputs with me for this writing.

In this long journey, everyone extended their complete support by guiding me in my thoughts, words, passages, and pages, summing up my efforts to make a blueprint for this book.

In this 'Everest in Mind' literary journey, the persons who deserve special thanks to Dr Darla Venkateswara Rao, Dr Bhangya Bhukya, Dr Pramod K Nayar, Dr Damodar Reddy Pamireddy, who are professors by profession, for their suggestions and guidance after reading the book. Meenakshi Srihari has given tremendous support while editing this book.

We thank Dr R.S Praveen Kumar, Coach Parmesh Singh, Coach Sekhar babu, Malavath Poorna, Sadhanapalli Anand Kumar, and Mr K Durga Prasad for providing photos and information.

On the occasion of the release of 'Everest In Mind', I warmly thank Mr Vangipurapu Raghavachari, Mr Mannem Veera Ganga Anjaneyulu, and Smt Sai Lakshmi for their concern and guidance.

On behalf of Kasturi Vijayam, we especially thank all the great people involved, and we feel it was a great experience. Syed Mastan was a design officer in the Indian Navy working in Mumbai. We thank him for his guidance on this occasion.

Our heartfelt greetings to 'Gajjala Durgarao'(Vijayawada), a teacher and writer who entertained the readers by illustrating the critical twists to the story in the book and Student' Thekkethala Sunil Rohan'.

# Table of Contents

# Mountaineer's Thought

The highest mountain and valley are both parts of nature. In life, wisdom and human skills are necessary. In mountaineering. Physical fitness and mental toughness are very important along with knowledge and human skills. Sudheer Reddy Pamireddy called me from Malaysia and asked me to express my opinion about the English version of his latest book, 'Everest In Mind'. I rejoiced greatly while reading the book as a mountaineer. The feelings of happiness filled my heart.

Since 1997 have been a Rock-climbing trainer/coach and since 2012 started giving training in mountaineering. 2013, I've been a rock climbing and Mountaineering coach through our organization, 'Transcend Adventures.' My heart was filled with the thoughts of Mountaineering. Making it accurate, I became a part of Poorna and Anand's courageous journey to Mount Everest under the banner of Operation Everest 2014. From the day of the initial training days to the stage of their safe arrival back to thc airport of Hyderabad, I handled the responsibilities as the chief trainer. The incidents and memories followed by that journey were always cherishing and joyful for me. The life-changing incidents and humans are non-forgettable.

In the eight months, I was the children's trainer, we implemented many new thoughts through 'Transcend Adventures'. We became a part of hard training. Anand and Poorna shocked and surprised the world with their Everest summit in a short period of time and set the world record.

The journey of Poorna and Anand had a special place in my memories. Both of them had ascended not only Everest but also other peaks of the world. At that time, I didn't realize that I was training the wonderful kids who are going to shake the world by creating world records. Now I feel that they have become great personalities with their uniqueness.

They caught the attention of the world with their short-span summit. Though they hail from the oppressed sections of the society carrying the burden of pain, they lightened the lamp of wisdom in their hearts. They moved their lives with lightning speed. They proved that if the children of the oppressed sections of the society were given an opportunity, they would utilize the opportunity and prove their potential one hundred per cent. Even now, I feel the whole happenings like a dream.

The author, Sudheer Reddy Pamireddy, displayed unwavering attention and extraordinary dedication in writing this book. From the first day to the end of the expedition, he articulated the journey with every detail in an impressive way, as if he was present with the children personally. He poetically presented the book. Surprisingly, he also mentioned the minute details of courageous field of mountaineering.

The author clearly explains the training, selection, love and affection of the parents and their fears, the fears that surmount everyone when they take their first step, and the chances of failure. The atmosphere of the Himalayas, the dangers impending in the mountains, the plant kingdom of Himalayas, the incredible nature, the role of Sherpas in the life of mountaineers, and the experience of Everest Expedition were holistically and attractively attempted by the author to the readers.

Sudheer Reddy is a great researcher who presented this book with a unique thought process. The writer started this book with a greater purpose of searching for the truth, and he completed it with a clear vision. The author had designed every character in this book with the trait of humanity. The story engraved in the form of history is astounding. Dr. Ambedkar's dream, the active part of S.R. Shankaran, the efforts of Dr. R.S. Praveen Kumar was detailed very well by the author. The changed thought process of social welfare organizations was clearly described in this book.

Sekhar Babu-the trainer of Poorna and Anand, Sridharan-the wing

commander, ARJ Venugopalacharya-the yoga teacher, Banavath Surekha teacher - the escort to Poorna as she was only thirteen years old, Rallabandi Srilatha teacher, Roshan Gahatraj- the course director of HMI in Darjeeling was also pictorially presented and this effort of the author indicates his greater efforts.

The childhood of Poorna, which was presented from the perspective of the child of the tribe and the forest, creates a great impression and vibrations in readers' hearts. In describing the historical happenings of India and the history of the Banjara tribes, the author's historical outlook, research, and results were visible to the readers in this book.

I trained thousands of students. Many of them ascended Everest and other peaks of the world. The meticulous detailing of my part as a coach in this book made me feel that there was a coach in the author. Surprisingly, the author transmigrated into every character and wrote this book.

I never met Sudheer Reddy Pamireddy, and the phone conversations have not happened between us. But he wrote my inspirational part to students matching ninety percent in the training time. The readers of this book will definitely inculcate curiosity, self-confidence, dedication, and the heart's capacity at a level of the increasing fold. The writer immersed himself in the goal of the Everest Expedition. The words were not adequate to appreciate him.

The author of this book refreshed my memory with his mature style blended with narration and creativity. I'm sure it will trigger a spark of self-confidence and self-confidence in the readers to achieve the impossible. I hope the writer will accomplish this goal. I cordially congratulate the author on this occasion.

Parmesh Kumar Singh.
Rock climbing & Mountaineering Coach.
Hyderabad, Telangana, Indi

**Prof.Darla Venkateswara Rao**
M.A., M.A., (Sociology), M.Phil., Ph.D. Telugu
**Professor & Head, Department of Telugu,**
**School of Humanities,**
**&**
**Procter, Proctorial Board**
**UNIVERSITY OF HYDERABAD**
**Prof.C.R.Rao Road, Gachibowli,HYDERABAD-500046, T S, INDIA**

http://www.uohyd.ac.in

E-mails: darlahcu@gmail.com
darlash@uohyd.ac.in
**Mobile** 09989628049
09182685231
Office: 040-23133563/3550
http://vrdarla.blogspot.com

# Poorna's autograph – A signature of Victory

**"The opportunity has welcomed me among lakhs of people.**

**I have also got a chance to reflect on equality.**

**With your complete consent, send me with your cordial blessings.**

**I will come back safe with your blessings.**

**Please send me. I want to go . . . ."**

The thirteen-year-old girl, Malavath Poorna, uttered these words. She was going neither to a school nor picnic. She was going, instead, to scale the highest peak, Everest. She was determined to prove the capability of her people, none of whom had travelled that far. She had also wanted to prove that victory only requires perseverance and courage, but not caste, religion, and tribal differences. Sudheer Reddy Pamireddy's Everest In Mind is the story of such great courage of a tribal girl who suffered extreme poverty and willingly put her life at stake in this journey of success.

As per my observation, the author Sudheer Reddy Pamireddy is a great researcher, and the book's title indicates his high level of thought. He is a voracious reader of Telugu, English literature, and other sciences.

Along with these, history is his keen interest. Apart from reading, he is also skilled in the art of putting in words, the knowledge he gains from his readings, and interpreting the information gathered to his readers. In geographical terms, he might be living away from India. But as an Indian Telugu reader, spectator, and speaker, he has bonded very intimately and lived with that companionship. I am stating these from his words and reactions and as a listener of the voice of his goals. He had taken the most significant responsibility of putting off the fire provoked by easily triggered sections of the society, turning himself into a social visionary. In India, particularly in both the Telugu states, he belongs to a very financially strong section. It is the section that paves the path for either money-making or power-grabbing at this point in time. But in these circumstances, I'm looking at the author as one who is becoming the literary voice of the oppressed and also as the disciple of Dr. B. R. Ambedkar. I believe that this book was written as a part of that greater aspiration. I felt highly emotional and was choked when I read this book. Poorna came from a tribal Tanda family. I experienced the same feeling of Summit the seven peaks as Poorna had. I felt like I had been crowned on the highest throne through her. While reading this book, the experience of reading the history of a great adventurer surrounded by a fantastic world surmounted me. The writing style is a blend of history and novel. This would be recognized as a novel by literary critics if this writing pattern continued throughout.

Vennelakanti Raghavayya has written about the Yanadis and Tribal Criminal act (1871) in his book, and Dr D.B.Nayak has written about the Banjaras in his book. The writer has honestly cited these books and many other research-backed literary versions. Prior to this book, the victory of Malavath Poorna has already been made into Telugu, Hindi, and English movies. Aparna Thota has written ***Poorna: The Youngest Girl in the World to Scale Mount Everest*** in English, and its Telugu translation also came out. My intention here is not to review all these. After reading the book written by Sudheer Reddy Pamireddy, I felt that there was a significant reason for him to focus on her Everest Summit, though she scaled other peaks after 2014. So, I think that sharing my opinions on this book will pave the way towards understanding that reason.

The writing style of this book attracts the attention of every reader. The author describes an incident in Poorna's childhood, when she was lost in the forest, thus: "The shadow would race faster in view of his daughter's safety." In the forest described in this book, the trees, the birds, and animals and their behaviours are not easy to state, unless they are deeply observed. These narrations add to Poorna's lifestyle in nature and indicate her bonding with it. The father goes in search of his daughter. The narration of the following of the dove and the trees in the forest reminds me of the writing Athadu Adavini Jayinchadu by Dr. Kesava Reddy.

When Poorna summits the Himalayas, her deeper feelings are beyond incredible, and the author describes the inexpressible feelings of Poorna thus: "In the early morning, the sky was sparkling with the stars which were similar to blue gems. It would be better to go there and grab a few of them."

The earlier historians had not adopted realistic versions in writing the histories of the Dalits, Tribes, and Sudras. It was necessary that this lacking must be filled, and that completeness is visible in this book. The early historians ignored the Banjara tribes and their contribution to the nation. The way the author puts forward these facts through Devidas displays the historical temperament of the author, through which he is ableto stress the significance of writing the new real histories.

The description of R.S. Praveen Kumar, IPS Officer, who was responsible for shaping Poorna's journey of success, and his role as Karma Yogi had brought wholeness to this book. This is an example of the balanced attitude of writing by the author without being influenced by any political impressions. S.R. Shankaran, IAS Officer, has been presented by the author as an extraordinary personality and social reformer, creating a feeling of respect for the author in the minds of intellectuals. The above two scholars described by the author seem to have reversed their surnames.

In this book, the words uttered by the Coach drive away the despair in everyone and instil new confidence. I read his words many times and quoted some of them in my diary as well. If you read them, a new electrical energy flows through you.

• Capacity is a state of mind. If the conflicts of ordinary thoughts block our mind, new thoughts will not spring up to step into any new field, it is not important how much you know but what matters most importantly is the way you learn, followed by the creative progress attached. What we are capable of is also decided by the measure of our capability in doing the tasks that we have chosen. The world glorifies only those who believe entirely in their capabilities.

• First, one has to be enthusiastic and self-confident to inspire others. The person lacking curiosity and enthusiasm cannot induce these in others. The increased level of enthusiasm also increases the chances of success many times.

• What you see in yourself will be visible to others from outside. Whatever you feel eligible for will be yours. If you are determined to mount Everest, your soul makes many paths visibledespite all the obstacles. Your thoughts will make it happen.

The book is filled with many more inspiring sentences like the above quoted. Here, for me, Everest is not only a physical goal but also the echo of the aim. That is why the English title for this book also sounds apt. It implies that it was written not only for Poorna but also for despairing minds to whom Poorna can be an inspiration. This book was written to portray Poorna as the summit of inspiration for others. This is why I said that it was written not only for Poorna but also for others within whom the darkness can be driven away by the force of her light of success.

This is the success story of the experienced benefits of the energy and capabilities induced by Yoga, Meditation, and Surya namaskar. Though these were already displayed by India earlier, it remains as a scientific version to those who feel them as a part of religion. These practices are important in the region of the Himalayas and its surroundings. That is why meditation practitioners are prevalent in Nepal, Tibet, and

China. As Buddhists follow them as a part of their peaceful living, they might have stood strong there for a long time.

Incidents showing Poorna taking permission from her parents for her mountaineering expedition, her mother's love, and her father'scourage will melt the readers' hearts.

As Poorna climbs the mountain, the levels of oxygen drop, she cannot walk anymore, and she thinks of her mother. Her family is in her mind when she has to eat to overcome hunger. When Poorna asks her mother about what she should bring while coming back, the situations and contexts make the readers emotional. The readers are sure to be as emotional as her mother, who replies that her safe return is her only priority.

Is it simple to mount Everest? How many Sherpas had lost their lives during this journey? Many from different parts of the nation lost their lives in this attempt. Poorna had seen the corpses of many during the time ofher summit. Was it possible to move forward knowing all this? Both Poorna and Anand were kids. If they attempted to climb Everest at such a young age, then the chances of possibility had to be carefully examined. If this had gone wrong, R.S. Praveen Kumar, who was highly educated, wouldbe blamed for this whole attempt.

R.S. Praveen Kumar constantly monitored them through phone calls. A sudden incident of Sherpas' deaths while helping mountaineers shook the Nepal Government, worrying Praveen Kumar about Poorna and Anand's safety. Their lives were more important when compared to the conquest of the Everest and he suggested they come back. Through the narration of such incidents, the author clarifies that Praveen Kumar took the utmost care during the expedition.

The author has also described the kids' response in this situation to show that they believed and followed SWAERO's principles, showcasing their self-confidence. "I am not inferior to anyone" is the first principle of SWAERO and inspired Poorna to aim to climb the Everest. "I will finish what I had started" is the tenth principle, which gave Poorna her confidence. This was why she was able to set the record as the youngest girl to scale the Everest. IndiGo Airways had imprinted Poorna's name on their airways as a sign of woman empowerment.

The author ends the book in an inspiring way. After climbing the Everest, Poorna displays her gratitude to Dr. B.R. Ambedkar, S.R. Shankaran and R.S.Praveen Kumar. This ending is a sign of the author's skilled narration. If you want to know it, you have to read it.

At last, the 'Author's Note' added is also thought-provoking and inspiring. If you read this excellent book, you will congratulate the author, Sudheer Reddy Pamireddy, along with me. Before ending this note, I would like to say something more.

While reading this book, I felt like jumping up and caressing her like a father. I feel like climbing when Poorna was climbing. I also feared that the despair at the end would take away her victory by the breadth of a hair. My heart lightened after she hoisted the victory flag.

The happy tears flowed down my cheeks.

I cannot climb Everest in my life. I cannot caress her like a father.But I can take her autograph.

I wish to imprint that autograph in myself as a sign of victory.This is the 'Everest In Mind' of this book.

Prof Darla Venkateshwara Rao MA., MA., (Sociology), M.Phil., PhD.
Professor& Head, Department of Telugu,
School of Humanities, & Procter, Proctorial Board
UNIVERSITY OF HYDERABAD

KASTURI VIJAYAM
3-50,Dokiparru Village -521322
Krishna Dist., Andhra Pradesh, India
Ph: 95150 54998
E-Mail : Kasturivijayam@gmail.com

# Poorna-The Power Peak

The force of self-strengths must drive life or travel. But the self-doubts of what might happen and might not happen will only hinder the prosperity of life. Is it possible for living beings who are poverty-stricken and who have not dared to think, in either thoughts or dreams, beyond the boundary of home, to gather the courage to utter "Mount Everest"? Can the courage go beyond merely uttering these words? Can the thoughts travel beyond the point of the dream to reality? What is the probability of this possibility? A tribal kidwith no basic amenities of food and shelter had filled her heart chambers with a destination mightier than the summit. She wanted to live her life of deprivation by attaching it to the Everest. She wanted to breathe life into the icy winds of the Everest through the air of her lungs. Poorna, with the sweat of her clay-soaked feet, wanted to make it Bindi on Everest. She vowed to turn the Everest into a frame for the untouchable heat rays that have plagued herrace for centuries. Poorna smashed the swinging steel cage of poverty with herdetermination and willpower and gave it life and respect with her strong mark of victory.

Some voices are meant to tell history. Some footsteps are designed to create history. Some passages of time are intended to create history. Some lives become light in the lives of lost hopes. Malavath Poorna's birth stands for such uniqueness. Birth is not new to the world, and no death is its end. We are all equal before the laws of the universe. But the heroes of history are different from everyone else in the way they customize their lives. The paths of change always welcome everyone. The passengers on this path must possess the traits of courage, alertness, adventure and patience, and they will make every change respond to you.

The person who thought of writing about Poorna, born in the remote region of Pakala, is not a simpleton. Despite staying away from his motherland for a long period, every cell in Sudheer Reddy Pamireddy is filled with love for the mother nation. Prior to this book, he won the hearts of readers through 'The Thought, A Journey of Seven Generations'. The present book, 'Everest in Mind', is written with meticulous discretion and capacity that it can attract the attention of world literature.

In the days of growing self-importance and self-recognition, Sudheer Reddy has taken an interest in the victory of a girl from the 'Banjara' tribe and felt it was his personal and national victory and shared some detailed information about Banjaras.

For ease of reading, this book is divided into seven chapters. Every chapter makes the readers thoughtful, fills them with confidence, and drives them to the goal. I want to brief a few aspects described in 'The Insightful Experience' by Padmaja Pamireddy. The happiness and sorrows might be the same, but the reaction towards them varies across people according to their traditions and customs. It is also reflected in the way they express their experiences. This displays the way the author looks at society.

The conversation between Poorna and her mother during the time of her climbing the Everest reflects the emotional and mental conflicts that wet the eyes of the readers. These tears flow through the abyss of poverty. On the other side, it will make us mount the heights of the most extraordinary summit. The beautiful sights of China, the feasts, the charming Tibet, the twists and turns of the Qingjiang River, and Poorna's struggle with her companion, the ice, are all well described in this book.

The chapter, 'The Ladders to the sky', recounts the incidents on 24$^{th}$ May 2014, when she begins to step towards her goal and leaps forward at the speed of thunder - a sign of courage in the hearts of the oppressed.

This victory was not the victory of Poorna alone. It was the victory of the lives spent within the boundaries of fate and societal pressure. It was also the victory of the sons and daughters of nature who make this world green. Also of the farmers who feed the world and the efforts of the history pillars drawn by labourers. This was also the victory of the mothers who sacrificed their lives to bring a new child into this world. This was not limited to a few sections, but to the united oppressed sections, standing as a flag of pride. It was a blood-stained flag that stood for the victory of all powers. Deaths due to hunger are common in poverty-stricken families. It is not difficult for them to sacrifice their lives for the sake of a great goal. The hunger of a poor girl made 'Malavath Poorna' stand at such a great height.

At last, the author Pamireddy Sudheer Reddy presents the steps, difficulties, learned experiences, self-experienced feelings, thoughts of the reader and everything else that made his 'Journey to Everest in Mind'. The author intends for the book to be a source of inspiration for forthcoming generations. I hope this book turns into a Veda for the low lives who are fed up with failures and fatigue, and I believe it will happen. I heartily congratulate the author, Pamireddy Sudheer Reddy, for the efforts and pains he has taken to make this book a possibility, and I hope it reaches everyone.

Dr.B.NagaSeshu
Assistant Professor

# The Insightful Experience

The road less travelled is chosen as her life's purpose by 'Malavath Poorna.' But Poorna is not the first one to choose this course of life and will not be the last either. Then why does her journey have a marked significance? What has she achieved in this path? To what extent does she, in terms of age, require name and fame? What is the goal of her life? Who have been her constant supports in life? Why were they on her journey? Why should we know about Poorna?

There is a reason. Poorna's mountaineering journey makes us travel into many unknown inspirations, life-giving paramount powers, the thought process between the goal and the achiever, and experiences beyond physical and mental states, which can only be felt after knowing her life. Nature is a secret to experiencing love and understanding and for a few, it is used as the tool for this purpose. Finally, a person's thoughts, opinions, beliefs, and experiences make the selections and eliminations. Among humans, there is a unique kind. This kind dedicates their lives to risky journeys. Their journey is as per their soul's command which is also their clear conscience. Their utmost alertness and awareness make them an integral part of nature, a part of the world and then also a part of themselves.

The journey to the Everest is the summit of the greatest peak despite the awareness of hundreds of hurdles awaiting in the middle to grab one into the abyss. It is not easy to go to the Everest. At a height of 8,848.86 meters, the air pressure decreases to thirty per cent and the temperature drops to minus sixty celsius. The more challenging task ahead is survival in the strongly blowing winds.

The knowledge of happiness is beyond humans. The hundreds of traditions do not separate happiness from sadness but their expression varies with the time and the meaning that behold the experience. The present generation of humans gets overwhelmed by the surface, ignorant of the fact that happiness lies within.

The quest for the answer to the primary question of the purpose of our existence makes us cross any hurdle and face any challenge in life. The surmounting obstacles and their crossing stage appear invisible after their purpose is served in life. On the other hand, wealth and peace will finally turn into discontentment if the purpose is unknown. Inspiration is an inner force of ignition. In life, the steps taken towards the goal garner more significance than the destination reached. People-oriented towards a productive life never accept defeat. Depending on their age and their financial strength, they make their journeys to experience the world. It is the tendency of humans to take bigger steps once everything is safely set. Then they start as groups with the slogan 'One life to hike mountains' with their aim to mount the seven highest peaks of the world.

***

In history, everything is a crossroads. The study of the society educates us about native beliefs. To know about any region, it is important to know about its culture. The beliefs built on personal orientation are futile in terms of a structural understanding of the country. The pages of history are filled with natives and immigrant rulers and the conflicts affecting the natives' connection to nature and their beliefs. India's nativity was destroyed by British rulers. Surprisingly, India's population was twenty crores and the foreign British number was slightly very low at that time. Finally, the suppression and domination of the British over India created a possibility for a one-sided history version.

There is neither a favourite story nor justice in history. The historian's understanding and version become history. Irrespective of one's likes and dislikes, imperialism is a political transformation. The majority of the cultures are brutally destroyed by the military, losing their form. The lost and the suffering fight to be victors, and sometimes they win with tact and discipline. As the sown seed transforms into a great tree, Poorna has sown a greater aim in her heart. This book 'Everest in Mind' is a sign to the discriminated section whose growth was oppressed by the partial laws.

--Padmaja Pamireddy

Base Camp, Tibet
Mt Everest
Tingri, Tibet
Southern Himalayan Valley
Himalaya
Khatmandu,Nepal
Mt Renock
Bhuvanagiri Gutta
Tiger Hills Darjeeling
Pakala Village
Tadvayi School
Poorna's Journey

# The Shining Diamond

The overcast sky settled under the verdant hills diminished the intensity of the sun dissolving in the cloud's shade. The predictable rain-driven wind tuned the tree branches to the music of nature. The springs of the hills turned to canals indicating that change is the driving force of life. The Beedi leaves, which have been the lion's share of income for Aadivasis for a long time, have kept the mothers busy gathering these, encouraging their children to follow their free will in playing. Children made themselves spectators to their mother's work by either passing time and drinking water from the nearby canal or playing as they wished. A little girl had become a joyful time-passer among them with her playful acts and utterances of no meaning. The peacock's dance in the far east direction distracted all the children and they followed along, leaving the joyful girl behind. Except for the girl of joy, the other toddlers rejoiced in the dance's beauty and grace and later reached their homes (Tanda), not mindful of the left girl. The busy nature of her work made the girl's mother think of the day like any other when her daughter would be home with the other kids.

After reaching home in the evening with the leaves collected for the day, Lakshmi searched for her daughter in the two rooms of the house. The girl's absence alerted the mother, and her inquiries with the other kids did not give her any vital information except for the details of the peacock dance and leaving the girl behind. The news of her baby left in the forest crumbled Lakshmi into pieces of fear. The consolation of the neighbours worsened Lakshmi's already fearful mind. Devidas, Lakshmi's husband, heard everything about their daughter from his wife's sorrowful tone after returning from the farm.

The pre-sunset in the west had paved the way for the sunrays to reach the open houses making their residents feel the warmth. The warmth added to the fear in Devidas's mind. The hapless thoughts about his daughter's whereabouts turned centripetal and centrifugal, taking a form in his body through the tense and fearful gestures of his jaw clenching and palms pressing. His steady walk stumbled in fear, and his mind is racing with all the possible thoughts about his daughter.

The dangerous disposition of the forest created mixed feelings of hesitation and resolution to find his daughter in the father's heart. The incertitude of the daughter's location and wild animals' cruelty speedened up the decision-making. The baby's cry can only guide the mission of searching, but if danger stirred up in between, the daughter's life might turn precarious. The thoughts of his daughter surrounded by wild animals in the forest and the lonely experience she would go through had driven him to the forest with a knife.

The day was getting darker, and the heavy-hearted father took his steps into the forest, immersed in thoughts about his daughter. The giant steps alerted the frogs in the canal to take leap away. Devidas freshened up in the channel ahead, twisting the turban towel with water, washing the face and neck, and checking the knife to ensure its presence.

Nature marked the day as the third day before the full moon, and the moon came over the grapefruit tree, and the wind was getting colder. There was a sandy way between the sunflower plants, and Devidas was only sure of his shadow in front, and the quick leap of the shadow was cautious of his daughter's safety if it was soulful and the shadow which was moving fast with Devidas, appeared to be more cautious of daughter's safety as if it has life. The path was deserted and the sound of Devidas's footsteps was getting more and more audible with the passing time. The anxiety mounting minute by minute, his eyes became sharp identifiers of the surroundings.

The forest is home to many creatures and Devidas thought that some of them may know about his daughter. A lizard in the bark of a tree created a spark in his thoughts about his daughter. But Devidas's thoughts circled around to wild animals like the boars which are a strong display of cruelty and cannot understand goodness like the predator whales in the sea, which only think about their forage, unmindful of their divisions. He prayed about his daughter's safety and moved forward, uttering 'Ambhi,' his mother's name and sobriquet of his daughter.

*Image Source from Nizamabad-Mallaram Forest Archives*

Strange noises surrounded the forest. The forest's origin and end were indistinct due to the undergrowth, bushes, and trees. Devidas can recognize the presence of natural forms from their own sounds. The moonlight's reflection on the hills, grass, and bushes could be foreseen by Devidas. The forest was in slumber, but Devidas increased his pace and turned his walking to running. The exhaustion in Devidas was evident in his gasps. A canal stood in the midway of the pathway. It stopped him for a minute, but his daughter's thoughts made him take a sprint into the canal as well.

Nature is strange, and it holds its secrets in its sleeve. Nobody can be certain of the number of generations witnessed by the forest. Devidas had been an inhabitant of the tribal area for twenty-five years. He had unique experiences every day with the forest. The forest's harmless hens had been his friends, and his life was built on the collection of Beedi leaves, honey tree flowers (Mudhuca Longfolia, Ippa), and feeding cattle alongside protecting them from wild animals. On the journey, he had seen rabbits, deer, bears, wild sheep, boars, and tigers as well.

A hissing sound from the bushes alerted Devidas to look around. A snake was shedding its skin in a bush and hitting its head on the head of the bush. On the journey ahead he saw two mongooses feeding on the grains. The mongoose pair reminded him of the snake he had seen before and he wondered about the dangers the forest could hold. Devadas's presence cautioned the mongooses to return to their shells of privacy.

Calming himself by placing his hand on his chest, Devidas moved through the dangerous forest. The thought of his daughter in such a dangerous zone created panic in the father's heart. Thoughts about her location and situation added fuel to the panic. He had walked far, and a sound in the north alerted him to turn. Bats flapping their wings, resting on trees.

Devidas shouted for his daughter in the vicinity of bushes, mounds and trees. The poignant time turned stick to snake, and the little snake curling despaired Devidas. The itchy sensation of the leaves turned blind on Devidas, and his five senses lost their natural abilities, and focused only on his daughter's safety. The rosary pea bushes were ripe, and the seeds are brightening in the moonlight. A sound in their direction alerted him. A pair of rabbits jumped into the bushes. He saw them till they vanished

The forest had plenty of rabbits. They are kings of running. They intentionally divert their predators in the wrong direction. Every animal will have obstacles with certain aspects. The rabbits are fearful of fences, and a small fence would numb them, and they stop and start licking their knees in a hapless position. Devidas remembered an omen: If the search for anything in the forest leads to rabbits fetching, it indicates a good omen that the searching object or person will be found. This thought filled Devidas with happiness as it appeared to be a good omen.

After walking for some time, a dove's cooing was as clear as fingers snapping at clever people. The dove never thinks of being silent. It tends to pass on the information it knows. It's a universal symbol of knowledge. It easily spots the missing birds and animals in the forest. The basic instinct of a dove is curiosity. It coos continuously if it comes across any new creature in the forest. The Dove enlightens the forest with its knowledge of wonders and findings. If it is imprisoned in a cage, it saves other animals from being caged by cooing. It is an enemy to the forest foxes which hunt in hiding, as it catches such sights and makes it clear to the fox's prey.

The dove's coos came from the northeast, and it created hope in Devidas's heart. He climbed a Vegis tree by adjusting his waistcloth and strained his ears for any clue. The dove was cooing from the white sage tree, and without a second's delay, Devidas jumped from the tree and walked towards it. Paying rapt attention to the dove's coos, Devidas continued in the tree's direction, and as the time flew the coos became more audible. Devidas was all ears and stopped his breath for a while to learn about the dove's findings. Standing on the stone patiently, the black dove flipped its neck and cooed continuously. It usually follows its instinct to show its new findings to the world.

As the mirror never lies, the Dove had done her duty, and the girl was sleeping under the tree in a hub of fallen leaves. Devidas relaxed after seeing his child. The dove who is helping hearted by birth brought him to his daughter, and Devidas felt indebted for its help. The child seemed sleepy, but the tear marks on her cheeks indicated that she got worried and cried before falling asleep. He took the girl in his two hands and came back home. The unexpected, safe return of the girl from the wild forest marked the blessings of nature on her and the fortune she was bearing. That six-year-old girl is **"Malavath Poorna."**

Devidas is a farmer. Besides cultivating his acre of land, he does electrical and cycle repair work. With years of effort, the hardworking and never resting Devidas couple built a home with a thatched roof and live happily. Lakshmi always strongly believed that her children will become famous in the course of the future.

Poorna has had little interest in food since childhood. The mother made Sorghum bread; Porridge and Ragi Malt are her favourites. Though lean by appearance, Poorna is always active in helping her mother. Collecting Beedi leaves with her mother is one of her likings. Along with that, collecting Honey tree flowers is also one of her easy-going routines.

Pakala Village (Tanda) is situated in the Sirikonda Mandal of Nizamabad district located in the Telangana State of India. As there is no provisions shop in the village, a five-kilometre walk is required to reach the nearby shop. The ever-working villagers always work happily on their farms. They constantly roam from place to place with the works scenario. The forest in the nearby surroundings made this village a spot of wandering for animals like rabbits, deer, boars, sheep, and bisons.

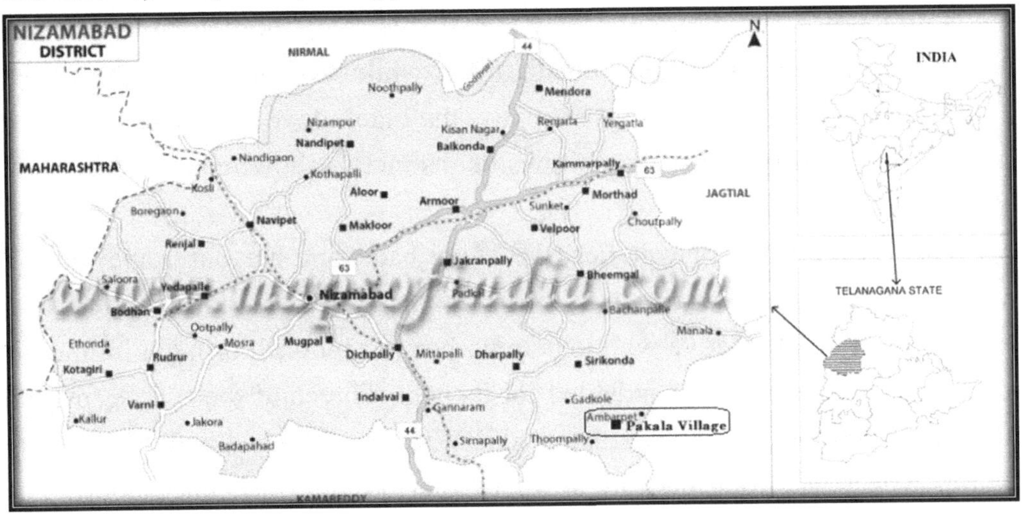


*Image Source from Maps of India*

After initiating her primary education in the nearby Anganwadi centre, Poorna started scribbling her learnings on the leaves and barks of trees in the forest, the collected Beedi leaves, the water springs, and the mud and on any surface which she felt suitable. Once, when Poorna was involved in writing on the mud, her father said, 'History remembers you when you do something remarkable.' These words of her father were imprinted strongly in Poorna's heart.

Poorna liked listening to the historical stories told by her father. As some of the historical incidents became interesting, Poorna would get deeply involved. "Why are we living in the forest? Why do these Tandas have more Banjaras? Who are we?" were the questions that tingled little Poorna when she asked her father. The answers given by the father made Poorna understand that her ancestors hail from Rajasthan and their profession is helping the military. As the story unfolded with many twists and turns, the children skipped their biscuits and encouraged Devidas to continue with the story.

The way Devidas narrated the story to his children displayed his greatest skills in expression; the flow of narration made it clear that it had been told many times before.

The state of annexation enjoyed by the patriarchal society never wants to come down and lose the taste of power. The civilized and uncivilized are enveloped by this structure. Rani Rudramadevi newly weaves this pattern. She fought endless harassment, rejections, and inexpressible hardships. Everybody thought of being ruled by the power of control.

History through many phases of time makes clear that women are considered an asset either to the family or to groups. Independence, financial strength, and ruling rights were not even dreamt of by women. Only the males could entertain the thought of ruling Kingdoms.

Until the eighteenth-century women were not considered beings with life and soul. Then where does the courage to rule arise in women? Modern American women got their voting rights in 1920 after several decades of struggle.

In India, in the thirteenth century, the woman who mightily ruled was Rani Rudramadevi. Having been born a woman, becoming a ruler had become a curse for her. During times when traditions ruled India, she outstepped them for a greater cause and stirred up traditional animosity. She leapt forward with great faith in the deity she worshipped, Kaakathamma, with extraordinary courage and determination. By spending most part of her life in wars, she protected her Kingdom.

"Woman as a ruler? Women ruling the Kingdom?" The questioning attitude of the feudal lords, her relatives, and the arch-rival Devagiri Maharaja were defeated by the actions of Rani Rudramadevi.

In the southern region of the Kakatiya kingdom, Rudramadevi's thoughts reached the sky. Surface-problems never frightened her, and her courage and adventurous spirit displayed the womanpower to the world. Her spotless rule won the hearts of people and set an example. Her rule uprooted the traditional patriarchal thoughts. She glorified the Kakatiya kingdom and extended the kingdom with Orugallu as its capital to Orissa, Karnataka, and Tamilnadu regions.

Those were the days the Sudras were the downtrodden caste. She made them her soldiers. She made inscriptions with the commanders' names and recorded their victories and contributions to history. Apart from promoting the arts and literature, she recorded their victories in history through inscriptions and took measures so that the history was not distorted. Rudramadevi allotted the ruling responsibilities of Sudras like Reddy, Velama, Nayudu, and Athi Sudras.

The main contribution of her victories was her trust in commanders. Recherla Prasadithya, and Gona Gannareddy were her trained commanders. She was an example of good governance to the succeeding Reddy kings and Vijayanagara rulers.

She dug the linked chain canals to provide water facilities to the Kingdom, which enhanced agricultural productivity. On the other side, she understood women and displayed her prowess of governance. Being a mother, she understood labour pains and made a law making a maternity hospital compulsory in every village.

Two walls on the outer side defend the highly protected Kakatiya fort, and the inner wall has been built on granite stones by Rudramadevi herself. Crocodiles and tigers freely roamed in the trenches built between the two walls. Soldiers were free to hike the wall by steps leading them to the top to guard the fortress. In the middle of the fortress, the temple of Kaakatamma, the kingdom's deity, had four engraved petroglyphs surrounding it.

Rudramadevi's name in history creates echoes in hearts, and her bravery ignites inspiration. Rudramadevi later adopted her grandson Prataparudra and made him the king of the Kakatiya kingdom.

In the cycle of time, some people's histories sparkle, some are enveloped by dusk, and their histories are a dark tunnel for the rest. The darkness is the kingdom of the strong. But history's survival is protected only when it walks in the light. The light makes the cultures of societies sparkle. History is destroyed due to many reasons. Among them, the ruler's role and the ways they are followed play a vital role. As the rulers change, so will the priorities.

Thousands of families from the Rajput kingdom were employed for military needs when needed in the Devagiri and Kakatiya kingdoms. Among them, a few guerrilla warriors were always prepared to play their roles when called for. As the life of the Banjaras is conjoined with wars, the Yadavas and the Kakatiyas had always chosen them to train the soldiers.

The Banjara's livelihood was to move in groups feeding their cattle when there were no wars. The Banjara's Tanda were usually a few kilometres away from the village and settled in forest base.

State security affairs always pose a threat to life. Working for soldiers of a state makes other states enemies naturally. These circumstances push life to a dangerous spot.

During the reign of Jalaluddin as Sultan of Delhi, the freely wandering Alauddin desired to become the Sultan. To unite against the Sultan, Alauddin needed army support and large amounts of money. To gather these, he made continuous attacks on the wealthy but weak town Bhilsa in 1293. After looting it, he surrendered the town to the Sultan to gain his trust, and that trust- winning factor drove the Sultan to make Alauddin, the Governor of Avadh, and the warfare minister as well. To fetch the additional benefits of another wealthy neighbouring town near Bhilsa, Alauddin requested additional troops, and the request was immediately accepted to conquer the Deccan region. Jalaluddin sent the army himself.

With the support of the army sent by the Sultan, Alauddin conquered and looted the Devagiri kingdom, skilfully routed the wealth to his placc, and requested the Sultan to collect the wealth by himself. The Sultan, when he arrived, was killed with a cunning ploy by Alauddin, and later he used money as a pawn to make the people from Devagiri to Delhi a part of his army.

After Devagiri, Kakatiya appeared as a money spot, and the Turushk army started efforts to conquer it in 1310. Though the Turushk army was equipped with the machines directing the large stones and the hay-lit fire targeting the enemies, they were unable to reach the outer wall of the Kakatiya kingdom for a month. The defeat and despair provoked them to burn the villages near the kingdom. Besides they also massacred the elderly and the women.

Slowly, with the help of slingshots launching large stones, the Turushk army conquered three towers of the Kakatiya kingdom at night. With the succession of three days, the Turushk were able to make the outer wall their victory sign. Finally, Prataparudra called for peace to save the people's lives and the kingdom. As an agreement of peace, Prataparudra offered a hundred elephants and ten thousand horses; the gold and silver were carried on thousand camel humps. Kohinoor, the most valuable 793 carat diamond, was also given off along with all these. The taste of wealth prompted the Sultan to attack Kakatiya twice in a span of eight months. Prataparudra was captured by the Sultan's army when he went to the battlefield to encourage his soldiers.

The last Yadava Ruler Harapala Deva's skin was peeled off when he was alive and shot dead and hung on Devagiri fort by the Delhi Sultans. Remembering this pitiful death, Prataparudra took permission and went to Narmada bank to attend calls of nature and disappeared into the river. The Turushk conquered the Kakatiya Kingdom. 'Andhranagari' titled Orugallu was changed to Sultanpur.

After Kakatiya's course, The Turushk eyes set on the southern kingdoms of the Hoyasalas and Pandyas, and they were looted in a similar way.

The story ended thus. The day had already turned to a dark night as the children's curiosity turned to questions. On Devidas's advice, the children finally went to sleep.

* * *

The results of research have strengthened the happenings of the story above. The study of the Banjaras of the whole nation can only offer valuable insight into their roots. Let's take a look at the research conducted on the Banjaras in a gist.

As per Dr.Vanne Gopal's research, Banjaras are located in seventeen states in India. They speak a language similar to thirteenth-century east Hindi, "Gori Boli", and this study was submitted to the UGC as a research paper.

As per V.H.Brahmanandam's research paper, "A grammar of Sugali language", the Banjara language was derived from the Indo-Aryan family, and the vocabulary of the Sugali language comprises multi-languages like Hindi, Punjabi, Urdu, Gujrati, and Marathi.

In "The Schedule Tribe", published by the Survey of India, the Banjaras arrived in the Deccan with Sultan's army. They served in the army and moved around carrying their luggage. Most of them returned to north India with the army of Aurangazeb, and the others settled in the south, surviving on cattle. A few made a nomadic living as per their culture.

# Wounded History

Christopher Columbus, the renown explorer, on the occasion of sending his first expedition report to the rulers, requested seventeen boats and 1200 warriors for his second expedition. The main intention of his expedition was to find gold in the Caribbean islands. In this process, Columbus and his men made the natives their slaves and made them work for them. They also imposed a rule to collect a certain amount of gold every three months on those who were above fourteen. The achievers were garlanded with copper necklaces displaying appreciation, and the ones who turned against them were punished brutally. If anyone tried to escape, they were haunted by hunting dogs and were killed by them, and this sport turned on a sadistic pleasure in Columbus. The tyranny and the brutality of Columbus's blood- stained history are not visible in any history book, but he is regarded as the greatest explorer who discovered America and is termed as the most courageous man in history.

Captain lieutenant James Cook, in 1770, following the British methodology of exploring, conquering, and mounting, claimed the Eastern part of the Australian continent. It was nothing but a death warrant to the natives and a sign of business and army looting. The jealousy, anger, pride, and wrathful nature of James Cook took many lives of natives. Aiming at thousand natives at once with arrows, he imposed a threat to their culture and existence.

By 1802, 10th April, East India with its cunning strategy in the name ofthe 'Great Survey of India', started dividing the natives. India appeared as a treasure mine to the British. Indian diamonds, silver storage, Elephant tusks, and forests seemed to be the treasure they were searching. As the creator Lord Brahma had four heads, so the English had two tongues to twist anything the way they want it.

Tavernier, a Frenchman, declared the Banjaras as "Maanaris" and stated that they have four trade divisions among them. Lambada supported the three Karnatic wars between 1745 and 1763 by supplying grains to the British army, which is recorded.

Najir Jung, the second Nizam was ordered on 15 November 1749 to provide for his army. Bussi, the French army commander took protection from Lambada on 5 July 1755. Bheema Naayak Bhangi's rights statement clarifies that the British used the Banjaras in the Mysore and Maratha wars as well.

After the 1817-18 Maratha Wars, the British army providence was taken care of by the British. The Banjaras had the revenue control over the central province and the Deccan plateau and conducted trading activities involving cattle.As the British wanted to take control over their independent trading, Lord Wesley ordered to levy heavy taxes on them.

Till 1850, the Banjaras transported salt in the country and in turn returned with cotton, grains, oilseeds, opium, fruits and flowers, and grass for feeding cattle.

According to writer B.G.Halbar, the Banjaras, who were supportive of the king's army by being messengers and army suppliers, were not liked by the British. The Banjaras' transportation and their cordial business relations with the kings irritated the British.

The Banjaras form their groups where they find their cattle fodder, and intime they gradually shifted to the Tandas. The Tandas are named after the head of the Tanda or their tribe's name, and they often spoke in 'Ghor-Boli' language. The Gor panchayats resolved their conflicts and declared solutions to them.

The historian T.R.Holnes described the first war of independence in 1857 as "The conflict between civilization and barbarism. History is a constant conflict between two groups. This is more visible in the Central Province. The sons of nature were constantly thrashed with the weapon of power, creating terror and pain in their hearts".

Professor Bhangya has stated that the necessary plate and glass are often thrown away, and the stones are stored. Similarly, in Indian society, caste-based occupations pass on from generation to generation. Selfishness always tends to be the social sense. The society's rules termed occupations based on caste.

Ambedkar stated, "An inspiring nation and morale booster ethics are not built on caste", making clear that caste-based occupations had not been responsible for any welfare of the individual or the nation. "Profession is the base of the caste's origin" has been stated by the social scientist Nesfield. But the concepts of caste and profession are different. If pottery is taken as an instance, this is hereditary. A man is born as a potter in a village and he dies as a potter in that village and is banned from working in other occupations. Except for agriculture, but agriculture without land is not honoured.

The British was terrified by the wanderer's attacks in the 16th century. This injected fear in them towards any nomadic tribe. Society was identified by agriculture and war at that time. A few castes took a safe haven in agriculture for food security, while others were inclined toward state welfare. The nomadic tribes carried out warfare and trained soldiers for the war. TheBritish recognized the trained tribes' number to be 500 and took the measures to oppress the freedom fighters under state treason. This created a threat to nomadic tribes. In 1871, the British passed the vital Criminal Tribes Act, implemented it all over North India, and extended it to the Bengal and Madras presidencies. They also extended it to their spouses and children. They brutally branded the children of these tribes as criminals. Later this law was hardened in 1897,1908,1911, and 1924 and extended to other regions and castes which were harassed. They justified their cruelty in the pretext of transforming barbarians into civilized men.

Nationwide protests began against the British, and people sacrificed their lives in many places. The Rajput's turned against the British in Varanasi. The tribals who unified and fought against the British were labelled as liars.

The Indian population was approximately twenty crores when the Tribes Act was introduced in 1870. Out of them, a six-crore population was branded as criminal, which implies that 30 per cent of the population were treated as criminals and abused. The accused and his family must take British permission to move out of the village and appear every day at the local police station.

The heads of the nomadic tribes sold their products to the outer world on bullock carts, and they never returned. Some of them were captured, others were killed by the British and the rest who went on the mission of finding the lost never returned. The dangers involved in this kind of living made them settle in the forests collecting firewood, honey, Beedi leaves, honey flowers, and selling bamboo baskets.

As per the sociologist Meena Radhakrishna, "The trade in the hands of British is equally creative and destructive. They passed the forest act in 1800. As per this law, the British prevented collecting firewood, bamboo, and grass, selling them, and feeding cattle. So, the tribes left their cows as they were not able to feed them on the hills. As there was no raw material the tribes lost their livelihood. Under the British influence, the people in the society gradually separated themselves from tribes like the Banjaras, Yanadas and Erukas. This was a clear statement to the tribes that they were not protected in any way. Along with the fear and the circumstances of loneliness, the tribes gradually forgot their skills, lost their courage, and remained with their natural trait of innocence".

The creation of history begins with cumulative perspectives of kingdoms, castes, winners, and leaders. When the rulers were ruthlessly destroying the nomadic tribes, the other sections of the society stayed away in the name of caste, feeling that nothing would affect them. When a sect of the society was destroyed, the remaining society had not displayed mass protest either in feelings or action. Though the British cruelly oppressed the nomadic tribes, the history is recorded from other perspectives, and the real story of the tribes remained dormant. In 1952, the Criminal Tribes Act was abolished.

The far-away mounds from the villages were distributed to the Banjaras in the districts of Medak, Nalgonda, and Nizamabad in 1975, and they cultivated them into productive farms.

Slavery is an imposed culture. But the society adjusts itself according to the consciousness of poor people. Freedom is the greatest cultural value.

The thoughts, beliefs, and actions of Banjaras reflect the Indian Culture. Indian Culture is not a single entity but an amalgamation of many cultures.

As said by the Padma Bhushan Awardee Vennelakanti Raghavayya, despite the manyfold stress, it is a happy fact that the Adivasis protected their language, dressing, songs, dance, instruments and festivals. It is the nature of the river to flow, and neither the dams nor obstacles can stop them from their flow. Similarly, the hardships imposed on the Banjaras had never made them give up their struggle for survival.

To protect and propagate the Banjara culture, there is a person named 'Bhat' in every Tanda. His responsibility in the Tandas is to take care of the tribe's culture and worship the seven mother goddesses, a tradition passed from the ancestors. Tholja, Kankali, Hingla, Mantral, Dholangar, Amba and Maremma are the seven goddesses.

As per professor D.B Nayak, the Banjaras are called, 'The Gypsies ofIndia." They are called by various names in various regions. Sirikiwala in Punjab; Gavaria or Gamalia in Rajastan; Lamana or Lambani or Lamani in Karnataka; Kangadia or Singadia Banjara in Maharashtra; Gahar, Gouria in Kerala; Banjara, Lambadi, Lambada, Sugali in Andhra Pradesh; Banjara, banjar, vanajara, branjara, branjvasi, labhan, labhana, baladiya, ladaniya in other parts of the country.

Caste is above the human, and emotion is above caste. The British decimatesd the feelings of Indians and brutally tortured the Banjaras.

***

The primary school of Pakala had a roof of broken shells. A screen of interlaced bamboo slats was covered around to make it a structure. Ten yards away, the dirt road integrated itself into the concrete road paving the way to Sirikonda. A tamarind tree marked the meeting of these two roads. A police vehicle halted at that tree. From it, heavily built people with starkly starched clothes, hats on heads, polished shoes and sharpened batons stepped out. Two or three of them had pistols. The black spotted dog near the school started barking. The only intention of the dog might be to indicate the forthcoming danger. The police officers rushed to the Tanda scaring the natives. To keep up the fear, they beat up the people on the way with sticks and batons despite there being no reason. They never thought of the bloodied and unconscious beings on their torture-mission. They just moved forward as if they were in a quest. The children were as scared as straggling birds in migrating flocks and hid in the slat of bamboo leaves. They were physically frigid due to the alarming danger in their vicinity, and they were trembling like wet squirrels.

A primary school teacher came to check the new arrivals out of curiosity. The children answered her unspoken question with the word 'Police.' The children had been brought up with fearful stories of branding children of that tribe as criminals in the womb since many generations.

The police brutality of scolding and thrashing is only for criminals and not for the innocent. The innocent should not be scared of the police. But Praveen Nayak was scared of them. He sat beside Poorna. Aadi Narayana Snacks shop was empty that day. The black crows were cawing for their daily feeders, the school children at the centre of the snack.

Poorna turned from walking to sprinting on the mud road. She left the books on the way. She was sweating all over, and her legs were trembling.Her ribs were quivering. She crossed the dirt and concrete roads, the canal of Pakala, and the surrounding small mounds and finally, tiredly reached her mother who was working in the field. Lakshmi was occupied with drivingaway from sparrows and peacocks by making sounds with an iron box. Devidas had gone to the forest in search of Madhuca.

After the head of Tanda, 'Bhat', heard of Poorna's experience, he made it clear that all these had been common to them for centuries. 'You were terrified of the police. As per the present changes in society, there is no scope for such fear. If the fear increases, it will lead to developing shame in the body. All of these will develop into a hesitation to move forward. This will set itself right in two days", he consoled Poorna.

"The law works on the people who are involved in evil thoughts and deeds. If fears make you run away from life, then life responds accordingly, and things also happen as per it. The sight of a green forest creates happiness in the heart. At present, in this nation, the modified laws are favourable to the Adivasis. If our thoughts are good, we receive respect and love from them. You think and act." With these courage-filled words, he bid farewell to Poorna.

# Studies Under Shankaran's Shade

Ashram Schooling is the best option to educate the children of remote tribal areas, make their lives meaningful, and inculcate dedication and determination in this journey. After completing her primary education at Anganwadi Center, Poorna enrolled in the Tadvayi Ashram School for higher education. The walls of the dormitory were filled with the paintings of Mahatma Phule, Dr B.R. Ambedkar, and S.R Shankaran.

It is not easy to have a happy childhood and a suitable environment for studies. The initial days at the hostel were uneasy for Poorna. The hostel food served was deficient in nutrients. Despite these difficulties, hostel life was hope for Poorna under her circumstances of darkness.

The school was two kilometers from the hostel. Green fields surrounded the hostel, and the golden-hued verdant environment was filled with the tranquility of nature. The children reached their schools touched by nature. Though the surroundings were pleasant and offered peace, the hearts still bore discomfort.

The ear-splitting speakers and strident sounds from the nearby temples and mosques surrounded the nearby area of the hostel. Some of the hostel children were playing with the old tires while others were playing a game of piling stones and bricks one above the other. A few were tearing the pages of the old books and flying them in the air as planes. Children separated from sports in their childhood will lead a life of flies in the mucus in the future.

The slum people living near the hostel had a simple routine. They laboured the whole day and earned their living. They ate and drank, were present-day oriented, and never thought of their futures. A new thought, a new goal, and a new revolution never struck them. In such a context, how can a new beginning arise? Their surroundings naturally prevented them from thinking differently from their routine. The oppression since generations had injected them with helplessness and surrendering.

The nomadic tribe's world is different. Fear always impends over them, and they spend their lives in pain for the conflicts they face. The hopes and lives of the forest children were gulped by the greediness and anger of the ruling section. Losing everything, they were left with grave silence.

The gap between imagination and reality is unbridgeable. We are Indians. We must unite and help ourselves from falling in every aspect. The scheduled tribes account for only seven percent of our country's population. But twenty-two percent of them live in prisons. They are not criminals but are pushed to that level by opportunists. Nobody is born criminal, and it is impossible for anyone to live with criminal thoughts their whole life. Dr. B.R. Ambedkar states that "Crime is a contagious disease and can only be treated by the love of the society.

The caste system, untouchability, superstitious traditions, disparities and inequality are all faults in our system. Their causes are deeply rooted. In the past, Charvaka and Lokayats made efforts to correct them. Sometimes in the process, the problem turned around to square one.

"The undermining consciousness and the decades of injustice must be prevented, and society must stand with lower order", stated Ambedkar. He took a leading step by guiding the 'dos' and 'don'ts' in society as a leader of the revolution. Ambedkar initiated the education and basic amenities provision in the reservations in the constitution to bring a change in lives of the depressed castes.

Human life is centered around beliefs. The traditions, customs, past history, and future thoughts revolve around these beliefs. The magic of society lies here. Societal conditioning happens under the shades of customs, traditions, and cultures. The aspects we witness and hear often become our reality. When that reality shatters with the hidden truths of facts, the change is considered a damaging pattern to society.

Our eyes are blinded by the layers of belief. The visible conscious changes are not accepted by our brain, conditioned by the layers already covered. The behaviour developed with the caste never vanishes. The years turned into decades and centuries are always visible to these constant thought and belief patterns. The dangerous happenings also does not change the people to think in the perspectives of philosophy, history and science. If this change happens, the coiled snake of discrimination flees from life.

After witnessing the negro labourers being sold in the market, Abraham Lincoln was determined to abolish Negro slavery by becoming the future president of America. This thought turned into a strong will and became an action, and Lincoln became the president of America and abolished slavery.Ambedkar is similar to Lincoln in India. For any change to happen, it is necessary that one should initiate it, and the rest follows later. Humanity is recognized worldwide. The lowly treated sections will definitely be uplifted at a point in time. After summiting in life, the person's humility appears as a glorified persona of confidence. Such kind words of humility would uplift insecure souls. The humanity in the human can only shape a leader.

S.R. Shankaran worked with the attitude, "I am a human, and I respect others as humans. I am here to help others in my capability." He worked for the oppressed and gained their trust. He was only seen as the most strong-willed person.

S.R Sankaran

He rose beyond the levels of physical needs and money. He dedicated his life to the service of the poor and remained celibate. He declined the Padma Bhushan, the nation's greatest honour, and remained a true selfless being. Though his administrative category of Indian Administrative Officer (I.A.S) equipped him with resourceful connections and a luxurious lifestyle, he was inclined toward helping the oppressed. He lived as one among them. He was determined to change traditional thinking to the level of humaneness.

Working with the oppressed drives one towards their welfare. Shankaran felt that he was correcting the wrongdoings of the orthodoxies, and he was a great philosopher to look at his doings as his duty. He appreciated and encouraged the steps toward the prevention of poverty in society. He always strived for the eradication of disparities.

Meticulous thinking sharpens wisdom in humans, and it happened in the case of Shankaran. His humanistic thinking made him a common enemy to the people who were making a living with the disparities that exist in the name of culture and dharma. The real reformations began after independence. When Shankaran was the principal secretary in 1975, the Government created ITDA and focused on the tribes' problems. Schools were established in remote areas, and the Forest Acts were changed. Shankaran made education for tribes a reality. Shankaran took a stand on implementing the constitution by helping the oppressed sections of the society.

The social welfare school inculcated the power and commitment required for life in Poorna. Making the impossible possible and managing the time followed by its fruitful usage and observation had become part of her personality through this education.

Rock-climbing training were held at Rock climbing school in Bhuvanagiri to build confidence in students, and schools were sent notices. The main intention of this event was to bring out the courage and bravery in the classes. This was a five-day program. Poorna, who was already an active volleyball player, showed interest in this event. Poorna attended this event with other students. Students were trained for Climbing, Rappelling and belaying in this event. The training coaches, Parmesh Singh and Sekhar Babu, taught them the rope handling and the confidence-building required for the sport.

Poorna won the best performer award in the rock-climbing task, and this win made her more confident in her future. This esteem-building might be due to the prowess in the newly acquired skill. R.S. Praveen Kumar, IPS, the secretary to the social welfare residential schools, distributed certificates to the winners of the event.

Quest is the source of human desires. The quest rooted inside moulds the external behaviour. When progress is visualized, it inspires and strengthens the goal of life. Praveen Kumar tried to better the conditions of the schools run for the oppressed sections of society. His determined dedication and practical implementation made him unique from others. He can deliver the required planning to students. His arrival was responsible for many changes at the micro-level in Ashram schools. These micro-changes impacted majorly the external core for quick results.

We are humans and a part of society, and we learn habits from it. By understanding the interests and psychology of the students, they must be encouraged to choose their professional choice as per their skills and likings. Sometimes the change at the microscopic level may affect the entire life to take the biggest turn. Bhuvanagiri Rock Climbing increased Poorna's confidence and created a strong desire for many more achievements in life.

*Image Source from Rock Climbing School Bhongir*

The question of 'How to do?' will be answered by the hundred paths folding out in front. Confidence plays a significant role in the growth of a human. The belief strengthened turns the human into the highest area of strength. The confidence to reach the goal increases self-confidence, thereby igniting the energy to move forward.

Look at a human who moves forward despite difficulties. He possesses the unique trait of confidence to do anything, and that leads him to complete anything that he starts. We become what we think. We need to inculcate good behaviour in ourselves to become a personality of radiance and must always work productively with enthusiasm.

This world is ruled by thoughts. The raw material for thoughts is our memories. A person is defined as the embodiment of thoughts he holds. The strong control their heart, and the weak turn into its slave. The controlling thoughts driving the actions are mightier than a person's intelligence. Sometimes a small thought may yield the best results. Taking responsibility for thoughts is also equally important.

***

Streetlights were glowing around the school, and that light had become a playground for light worms. After her volleyball practice, Poorna freshened up and asked her drill teacher Sureka about Praveen Kumar. Surekha narrated the inspirational story of Praveen Kumar to Poorna.

There are many turns in Praveen Kumar's life. His perseverance and sensitive focus are incomparable. Though he is an IPS officer with the best results, he still diverted his focus to higher studies. This led him to join Harvard's Master's Program of Public Administration. The studies invoked the universal human spirit in him. The Harvard education filled new experiences in Praveen's life. His exposure widened.

Studies give strength to face any tornado and cyclone in life. With the cumulative essence of subjects like Social Studies, Anthropology, Philosophy, and Psychology, Praveen Kumar travelled back to India with new thoughts and clear consciousness. Praveen Kumar believes that time is most powerful, and he realized his purpose in life and willingly accepted the responsibility of Social Welfare Residential Schools. His humanistic approach made him the big brother of the schools. His thoughts are revolutionary and change oriented. He is always inspiring, abides by the Indian constitution, and is a human rights soldier.

Praveen Kumar changed the existing social welfare school's management from loopholes orientation. He strongly believes that the humanistic approach is more important for students, and he strived hard to eradicate poverty and inequalities. He prioritized the thoughts and ideas of children above all.

The orthodox who are never welcoming of changes always resist it and always look out for constancy. If anyone tries to make a change, then they oppose the change by justifying why thechange is dangerous. They also demand change in the oppressed people and complain of it being impossible for the downtrodden sections to adopt traits and make changes.

Researchers have made it clear that students observe their favorite teacher's habits, expressions, and attitudes. By the time Praveen Kumar took the responsibility for the schools, the schools' position worsened. The existing teachers' unions are blowing the whistle. If the teacher does not have the good intention of teaching, who will teach them? As per the regular custom, the paperwork and bills are perfectly misleading, and the hygiene and sanitation are neglected. Children are deprived of nutritious food. Opposing the working unions and setting the things right turned hard for Praveen Kumar.

In this system, a person's success or downfall depends on the environment. Though birth is not in human hands, caste, religion, tribe, and creed chase as soon as a person is born. Man cannot escape from them.

Praveen Kumar is aware of the fact that society is built in the order of top to bottom. If the rulers are changed, then as a consequence the ruled will be changed. If the oppressed section takes the responsibility of leadership, then the standards will improve, fills others with, and thatleads to adjusting for the more significant cause. Following this principle, Praveen Kumar yielded the best results in the case of schools.

The process to change the thought process of the oppressed has started. He formed the 'SWAERO' organization with the Gurukulam alumni. He created awareness about education among the parents and collected funds and he spent them on the welfare of the SWAERO students. The philosophy of SWAERO is the welfare of society. Praveen Kumar made clear the inequalities involved in the traditions passed on from the millennium. He took steps towards allowing students their free will in following their likings and skills. To sharpen students' skills in social welfare residential schools, he introduced chess and horse riding. He also introduced music and filmmaking training sessions.

No one is great by birth. The sacrifices and hard work pave the path for greatness. It is made clear by the lives of great personalities. Opportunities flow like waves in the sea in life, but the people who productively utilize them are eligible for greatness.

*Image Source from Siasat.com*

***

The loser always looks for the reasons for failure and is scared of tiredness. He spends his mental energy on thinking only about his fears about the future. He enlarges his problem every time, terrifies others, and derives pleasure from it. He bores others. It is better that a thing worns rather than rusts. The pessimist always thinks about his illness. It is usual to get a sympathy card for illness. But the friendship and respect are lost. Some mistake desire as belief.

Confidence can shake mountains. No one likes to be a second-class person and are not pushed forcefully to that path. Poorna let go of her second class-human mentality and embarked on a new journey.

# In the Vicinity of the Himalayas

"Common man generally overestimates the power of others and underestimates his own power. It's not important how strong we are, but it is important how wisely we solve a problem", the headmaster praised Poorna in the school assembly regarding the occasion of special appreciation for her from Praveen Kumar. The other children encouraged her with their thundering claps.

In an afternoon class, Poorna and her friends were painting on a T-shirt. Then the Physical Training teacher, Surekha, listed out the twenty students selected by the Himalayan Mountaineering Institute and clarified the program's goals. Among the students, Poorna stood as the best performer in the girls' category, and it instilled new confidence in her. "Everything will havea reason, and nothing happens lacking it. Never misuse the opportunity and new acquired recognition" saying so, Surekha affectionately tapped her head.

The arrangements for training the selected students proceeded at a fast pace. The students were glad to find that the training was going to happen in the snow hills of Darjeeling, especially since the selected students were going out of the state for the first time. Sekhar, the coach, visited the hostel and reminded the students about the required things and the precautions to be taken.

Creative thinking is nothing but looking for the skills to perform a task with higher potential, reducing the complexities involved. Working towards the victory of others is also considered creativity. With great thoughts, creativity, and inspiration, the company "Transcend Adventures" was established by Parmesh Singh and Sekhar Babu.

The parents of Parmesh Singh are Babulal Singh and Padmavathi. Their ancestors hailed from North India, and they shifted to Hyderabad. Babulal had rendered his services as an employee of HAL. Though their family background was middle class, Babulal had raised his son with the thoughts of making him a great mountaineer. Coach Paramesh was the teacher of Sekhar babu before ascending Everest. Their friendship with bounding.

Sekhar Babu is an Everest summiter. He is a great goal achiever. His father is an ordinary RTC bus driver. The generations prior to Sekhar Babu never thought of great goals like mountaineering. At the age of 26, Sekhar Babu mounted Mount Everest, and later, he dedicated 12 years to studying the depths of mountaineering. In 2012, by establishing "Transcend Adventures", he is giving life to the adventurous journeys.

The conscious spirit takes birth before the thought process itself. The conscious thoughts can only be controlled through our actions. The person having bigger thoughts will have the clarity for his future plan of action. Imagination is an added value to the human. The prior knowing of one's capabilities and awareness creates a roadmap to the plan and then success. The teacher first recognizes talent in a human. Sekhar Babu, as a teacher, has not seen the existing form of Poorna but the person she could become in the future. That is how the Everest Mountain journey started in Poorna's life.

***

*Image Source from Himalayan Mountaineering Institute*

On 26 October 2013, at 6 AM, all the selected students reached Secunderabad station with their baggage. For these adventurous mountaineers, the Railway department has added a special bogie. Carrying in it the excited children's laughter and games, the train raced ahead. Gradually the cold started. Due to the high air pressure in the Bay of Bengal, two bridges near Orissa collapsed. The train changed its route to Kazipet-Karimnagar-Nagpur-Madhya Pradesh and reached the New Jalpaiguri Station, running late for 52 hours. The children were tired of the journey, and by the time they landed, they suffered from body pains and fever. They reached the railway station to Darjeeling through taxis, where the temperature was 6 degrees celsius.

By 6 am the next day morning, the children were ready for training.Trembling in the cold, they waited at the HMI gate and entered it after being called. The instructor of HMI was surprised at the children, who were very much younger. "They were very young. Until now, such young children were not trained, and if the training impacts the lungs, bones, and muscles still in the developing stage, I will be held responsible, so I'm not willing to train them", the course Instructor, rejected the idea of their training. While coach Parmesh Singh was discussing this with the management, the children waited outside, worried about the special permission from the course director. Roshan Gahatraj (Jyothi Sir). His decision was completely favourable. It was fortunate for the children that Jyothi Sir was the HMI course director.

The atmosphere was cold. The mountaineering institute was surrounded by a botanical garden, a feast for the eyes. The birds were tuning to the music of nature.

The surroundings and the climate prepare the mountaineer's body for training. Coach Parmesh Singh suggested that the students make a 4-kilometre run around the institute's hill. Running in the hill stations generated heat in the bodies. The hiking helped them to adapt to the lowest recorded temperatures of that region.

*Image Source from Coach Parmesh*

As a part of the testing period, under the orders of the course director, the children reached Tiger Hill which was 2,590 metres above the sea level. The path makes its journey through the sky. They made way for a mongoose mother travelling their way with its two cubs. But the mongoose was scared and travelled back the way it came from. On the other side in the nearby valley, two white eagles were rubbing their necks which might have been their love language.

"Focus on the task ahead, all of you were brought here to rise to heights using the opportunity and not to escape with lame excuses. Taking responsibility builds recognition, and I want all of you to reach heights"; Parmesh Singh was inspiring the children while walking with them.

Though some of the children felt uneasy to acclimatize, they moved forward, keeping the uneasiness apart.

To keep the children interested in the sport of mountain-climbing, coach Parmesh spoke about the psychology of mountaineers.

"You can create wonders only if you are creative with your effort. What you see inside will be visible to you outside as well. What you feel eligible for will be what you achieve. If summit the Everest is your true dream, then despite any number of obstacles your heart will find a way to do it. Your thoughts propel the actions to happen".

Capacity is a state of mind. When our minds are stuck in ordinary conflicts, new thoughts never strike our brains. It is not important what one knows while entering a new field, but the intensity of learning after working in it matters significantly. The main learning being the attitude of applying the knowledge of learning with creativity. What can we do? How best can we deliver in the chosen field? These depend on the way we think about them. People who think optimistically are respected by the world.

Mount Everest's height increases every year. Similarly, if we enhance our understanding and capabilities, then we will definitely achieve victory. In the present times, only people who constantly work on improving their skills and capabilities succeed.

To inspire and encourage the other person, one must be vibrant and enthusiastic. The person lacking enthusiasm cannot ignite it in the other person. The enthusiasm in the work we are doing will yield the best results.

You may not be interested in the ice mountains. But if you start studying about them, then in the process, questions arise, like, "How are they formed? What is their height? Which crops are grown in the snow seasons?What is the lifestyle of the people living there? How are human relations formed there? How do their lives change during the rainy and winter seasons? What is the lifestyle of the Sherpas, the major tribes surrounding the Himalayas?" We observe an interest that is generated in the process of knowing these things.

By then, they had covered half the path of Tiger Hill. Parmesh Singh was moving forward without displaying any tiredness, and the children were following him.

Some look at history as a lively flowing wonder. The rest look at it as a dull and boring thing. Try to look at it rationally. The way you look at people is reflected by them as well in your case.

The more we dig into a subject, the more interested we will be in it. Nobody is born confident. Confidence helps to achieve a goal and becomes a milestone in the process. With a good attitude, build your confidence on a daily basis.

Your food intake decides your physical stamina and disease resistance. Good food enhances lifespan as well. For summit the peaks, physical health and stamina are most important.

On listening to all these, Poorna came running to Parmesh. She shared her experience of climbing Bhuvanagiri hill, which at first scared her, with him. Parmesh Singh smiled at her words and said that fear vanishes into thin air by trying hard. By looking at fear as a different thing from us, and observing it as a separate entity from us, the intensity of fear diminishes. Just follow your conscience and righteousness. Our conscience is a filter for rightful thoughts. It filters out the wrong thoughts in us through rational thinking.

People who think big will create great enthusiasm in their lives with optimism and possibilities. They try to imbibe the same in others. To make a profound impact on others, words and thoughts making such a positive impact must be used. The victories achieved in the history are first thoughts and then turned into actions.

Goal is an intention. Goal is a clear thought process. Goal is the result of intended actions. Goal is more significant than our dreamt dreams. Goal acts as an accelerator to move forward. The plan for the victory is driven by the goal, and the goal leads us to a clear path. In our life, both are significant.

Remembering the sorrows of life often nourishes the tree of hardships with the required nutrition. Conflicting thoughts grow in our lives and destroy our confidence, leading to great despair in life.

*Image Source from Coach Parmesh*

People full of negative thoughts always put down and find a way to punish themselves. They believe that everything that has happened in their life so far were only painful. They always find solace in darkness and despair and like living there.

If we observe carefully, we can find both happiness and sorrow in our past. But it is important which of them is prioritized in our life. If the painful and rejecting thoughts are forgotten and the happy ones are brought to surface, then it changes the thought process to positive. Cleaning the dishes in the kitchen after dining reduces the work. Similarly, destroying negative thoughts at an early stage is easy. Parmesh felt happy with the activeness brought out in the children by his words.

Winners can be easily identified by activeness in their work. The ordinary, the lost and the winners are differentiated by this trait. Lazy people are less active. The worker works and makes other work as per the plan and will be happy with the work. This enhances her confidence. This confidence builds her security and self-confidence.

The lazy person always procrastinates, and she always finds reasons for it. As soon as Parmesh Singh brought up the topic of laziness, the children playfully pointed among themselves who was lazy and moved forward.

Implement any thought as soon as it strikes you. Working on the thought at the earliest point in time increases confidence in the person. Do it fearlessly and enhance your confidence. Added to this, implementing a good thought into action gives immense satisfaction.

*Image Source from Printrest*

The children were climbing the hill while carefully lending their ears to Parmesh's words.

Parmesh started narrating the incidents experienced by renowned mountaineers earlier.

Once when I went to the Himalayas and visited the Kedarnath, and trek further higher to Vasuki Tal, The trainer there explained the bungee jump to us. “It is not difficult to jump from hill peak to valley. But the people trained to jump will also be under their heart’s control at that instant of the jump.They heed to their heart and fear the jump and return without doing it. While others, during the time of waiting for their turn, utilize that time to increase the confidence and courage required for it. And a few are scared at the thought of what danger might unfold during the jump and withdraw from it.

The excessive time spent on procrastination increases the terror and fear in the person. Remember that once you are involved in the work, fear disappears gradually. Working is the only solution to fear and anxiety.

The Kanchenjunga Mountain range is visible from Tiger Hill. The visible distance in the north is covered by the highest mountain peaks enveloped by ice, and behind the peaks are spotted white clouds. Among all the peaks, Mount Everest is the highest peak.

*Image Source from Coach Parmesh*

At the same time, tourists who came to see the sunrise on the Tiger Hill were watching the Mount Everest, which is 172 kilometres away, with their binoculars. A few women were coming with the hay on their heads. They were displaying their happiness to the world with their smiles and laughs.

The officer of the Himalayan Mountaineering Institute noted the time required for the children to climb and the physical changes that occurred during the climb and he completed the report to be submitted to the HMI. The children were able to tolerate the lowest temperatures. The appreciation for their efforts made them happy and encouraged them.

The oxygen level drops at a higher altitude. At that critical temperature, depending on the body type, sometimes conditions like Pulmonary Edema and water accumulation in the lungs may set in. But in this journey, all the children were healthy and active and experienced no such conditions. This victory led them to the advanced training to climb Mount Renock.

The children started climbing Mount Renock, which is 16,500 feet above the sea level from the mountain ranges of Kanchenjunga. The mountain ranges are curvy and the pits are half-open. Very carefully, the children with the help of ropes cautiously stepped on the stones and started climbing. A minor negligence on their part may result in breaking one or two bones. Only ice and peaks existed there. The sharpened edges on the black stones are sharp enough to pierce through the shoes.

The shining ice mountains fill the heart with pleasure. The sun's rays on the shining ice make the scenario breathtaking. The water flow mixed with white and blue makes ear-splitting sounds. On the other side, the wind blowing from the brittles on the ice makes the Omkar vibration, indicating the journey towards stunning yoga path. The land here is not suitable for any human to live. The continuous icefall deprives the opportunity of living not only from humans but also from other living beings. The ice-filled canal in between reminded Poorna of the canal in her village. The village canal is filled with fish, and the ice-filled canal does not have any living creatures in it. There is no sight of butterflies as well. The water is crystal clear here. The snow here makes everything appear as clear as a mirror for reflection. The stunning and breathtaking scenario is an eye feast.

Whenever the strong winds hit the canal's surface, the waves forming on the ice indicate an ongoing conversation between the air and the canal. The Renock peak was successfully scaled by all the children. All rejoiced at the beautiful sights on the peak. The atmosphere excited and energized them.

There was a Himalayan peacock resembling a hen on the Renock peak. The Himalayan Monal was brightly speakling with multiple colours and was very attractive. These birds come here to hatch their eggs. In this species, the male peacock helps the female in hatching the eggs.

*Source from Printrest*

Women's power is reaching peaks in every field to set an example to the world that they are equal with males in every aspect. The ice mountains filled Poorna with power and they sharpened her thoughts. Women, who comprise half of society, are always equal to males, and their progress will make the society do so as well. Thinking over this, Poorna made the return journey from Darjeeling.

There was a complete change in her thought process. She stopped looking at the fearful past and present. Now her thoughts were focused only on her future. She started thinking about making herself a better person. She realized the importance of new thoughts in improving the way of doing things. It is an undeniable fact that change charges humans to move forward.

Where will the journey of Poorna from Pakala, a remote village, progress? The little training experience has driven her to mount Tiger Hill and Mount Renock. What might be her strengths?

# The Goal of the Adventurous Journey

As per the orders of Praveen Kumar, the report was examined by HMI. Parmesh Singh and Sekhar Babu enlisted nine students for the Ladakh Winter Expedition following the report. They successfully completed this expedition with six out of nine students. The children learned the skills of walking in the snow and ice and spending nights in sleeping bags and tents at night during this expedition. This expedition provided an opportunity for the trainers to check the capabilities of the children.

Four students, Poorna, Anand, Satyarao, and Gangadhar, were selected and finalized after the Ladakh Winter Expedition for the Everest Expedition. The meetings and discussions with the government led to the final selection of two among the four students and the 70 lakhs fund was sponsored by the government. Poorna and Anand were on the final selection list.

***

Meditation with a single-minded focus on the breath brings success near. Research on meditating and non-meditating Mount Everest mountaineers was conducted by the Pavian University of Italy. The group that had meditated for an hour for two years before summiting Everest had high oxygen intake, and the area of the lungs expanded by 70 percent. Most of them did not require oxygen cylinders most of the time while summiting Everest.

Meditation increases the regenerative capacity of the body. It empowers the body to fight even under the circumstances of low levels of oxygen. The Italian mountaineer, Reinhold Messner, stated that he was able to reach the depth of 100 meters in water due to his meditation practice of focusing on the breath. This is called the 'science of breathing.'

Sekhar Babu, the coach, believed that meditation is the perfect means to create a balance between the body and the brain. Keeping it in mind, he created a physical and mental training schedule for Poorna and Anand, with the Yoga and Meditation teacher, ARJ Venugopala Charyulu.

Among them Yoga, meditation, and sun salutations were compulsory.

The daily practice of meditation opened a new world to the eyes of Poorna. At first, she practiced focusing on her breath. After crossing this stage, she became an observer and started seeing the changes happening in her body. She built a habit of creating awareness of each of her body parts. Somehow, Poorna experienced peace in the silence. She felt those moments of silence valuable. The ever-internal conflict slowly soothed. The mind-boggling questions, judgments, memories, desires, and uncountable thoughts vanished into thin air.

ARJ Venugopala Charyulu

Poorna made running her habit. Every day, she ran 25 kilometers efficiently. Testing the patience of the children, new estimates were under preparation. The non-sop running record was 31.4 kilometers. Poorna had not experienced any hardships though the practice at the gym toughened.

Truly speaking, the practices were many standards above the age of Poorna. But Poorna did all of them with her heart and soul. She tuned her brain above her age. Our brain behaves by vibrating with the frequency that we tune it with. Now Poorna's thoughts were tuned to the frequency of the Everest.

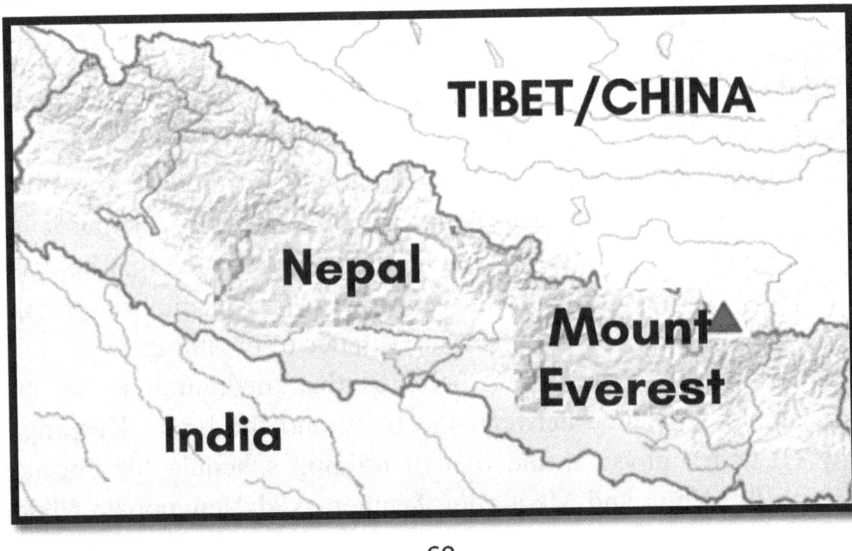

The essence of the Himalayas invited the sense of childhood. This might be a starting step for the spiritual journey of a child. Now the body and mind of Poorna were unified, and the unified thought was Mission Everest. The breath taken, the word uttered, and the action taken were preparing themselves for the mission of climbing the peak of the Everest. It might be the beauty of the Himalayas that attracted her.

The thermometer can only indicate a temperature up to minus 63 degrees celsius. It cannot display below this. Poorna studied the lifestyle of snow lives. She tried to deeply understand by studying more books concerning the Everest. There were two ways to climb Mount Everest. One is 5,364 meters above land level, located at the south base camp of Nepal. The other one is at an altitude of 5,150 meters at the North base camp of Tibet. Between these two, the north-camp route is difficult to make, and it was also the one which only a few mountaineers had taken to climb the peak.

Poorna and Anand were fed athletic food. Physical training teachers, Surekha and Srilatha were appointed to monitor them. The diet included milk, eggs, chicken, dry fruits, fruits and vegetables to strengthen their muscles. As Poorna was a little reluctant to eat, this diet intake was hard for her. The coach Parmesh took care of the training of the children, and the coach Sekhar Babu was busy with the preparation of the required documents.

***

Victory has many friends, but responsibility has only a few. The coach, Parmesh, is a lawyer, and he applied for the permission for the Everest Expedition on non-judicial stamp papers. As Poorna was only 13 years old that time and was a minor, the Expedition required two sets of declarations from her mother and father stating that they were entirely responsible for the expedition.

**"The opportunity has invited me despite lakhs of people waiting. I got an opportunity to stand for equality. Send me with heartfelt blessings. I will come back safely with the strength of your prayers. Please send me. I wish to go.**" With great courage, Poorna strengthened her parents with her willpower.

"Dear daughter, these adventures were not meant for us, and we were not up to it. But an invisible power was visible in your steps. We never will discourage you." Praying to nature, Devidas signed the declaration.

Lakshmi, the mother's face turned red. Her lips trembled. Her body was drenched with sweat due to stress, and she was in tears. She completely rejected the idea of sending her daughter on a dangerous expedition.

"This is a war between birth and death. This expedition definitely comprises danger and losses. They are not limited to our family. These affections will never end. The tears will never stop as well. Your only responsibility is to sign on the papers", Devidas consoled her wife.

Devidas's words made Lakshmi thoughtful. Slowly, she stepped towards her daughter, who stood like a pillar. "Dear! This was not the right thing to do. I do not like you going there. I am not ready for any sacrifices" pain enveloped the words of Lakshmi. Poorna's strength was limited to making her father understand her dream and have his approval, but her efforts were futile regarding her mother.

Devidas slowly approached them. "The mountains attract mountaineers like a magnet. The strong attraction and bond with the Himalayas in our daughter's soul are not accidental. We cannot stop this journey at this time. If so, we should have stopped it at the initial stage, when she climbed the Bhuvanagiri hills. If the Himalayas pulls humans to its side with its power, we are helpless, and the only thing we can do is pray to nature. Please understand," Devidas's words changed Lakshmi's heart.

With reluctance and under compulsion, Lakshmi signed the papers and prayed to her favorite deity, Hanuman. She held Poorna close and cried. That was the time when Poorna forgot herself. The mother's only concern was her daughter, as she was also part of her. Poorna felt that she was fortunate to have such parents.

***

In the name of modernity, the present generation of children are making their lives a running race which is turning into a lost race of time. If life is a journey, then the Everest's journey is equally significant. Education can only drive away the innocence of tribes' children, and it leads to creating a goal in life. This makes them think and act in the direction of equality. This is not only the success of the Everest Expedition, but it also signifies history's victory.

On 6 April 2014, the AP Express was ready to depart from the Hyderabad to Delhi in fifteen minutes. Poorna and Anand appeared like bows targeted to a goal. These child soldiers had aimed for something high, which had not been done earlier.

The future is uncertain, and there was nothing to lose in the present. The only thing in their hands was prayers. Relying on blessings, Devidas developed a belief that his daughter would return safely after the mission. Strengthening that belief, he was distributing the pieces of the coconut broken at the temple as prasad to all. Kondalrao, Aanand's father, was immersed in a discussion with Praveen Kumar.

**Poorna and Anand with Coach Sekhar Babu at Hyderabd Railway station**

*Image Source from Sadhanapalli Anand Kumar*

"Time is precious, and you handed your precious children to me, and they will return as winners" Praveen strengthened them with his words and bid farewell. Kondalrao folded his hands and said, "We for all", and the train started. Poorna peered out of the window of the train and bid farewell to her father.

***

The Tribhuvan airport of Kathmandu, which was considered the first step for Everest mountaineers. The runway lies between the hills. This was 1330 meters at sea level. Nearly a dozen fatal accidents occurred here in the past three decades. This area represents the motto of scaring, warning, and safeguarding. The Poorna team made their journey to the Everest base camp from this place. Poorna's goal was to scale 290 kilometers.

The surrounding black clouds appeared like black sacs carrying water to the sea. The ice-covered Himalayan mountains were multi-colored and twinkling. To adapt to that temperature, Poorna's team planned to have possible night halts during the eight-day journey from Delhi to the Everest base camp.

Poorna felt like she was being invited by the beautiful nature; and the whirlpooling water drops in the air. As the setting sun turned the ice hills golden. It was a feast for the eyes. Dudh Kosi river flowing from a significant height was energetic in her flow. The mica-filled stones were shining black under the hills. The lands turned for cultivation between green trees were laden with potato crops.

The exterior sounds became inaudible to Poorna due to the music of the flowing water. The strongly blowing north wind strengthened gradually. The high wind touching the bodies unshielded by coats was almost sharp enough to cut the body. As the slight shower turned into heavy rain, Poorna continued to her camp.

Nepal's cultural greatness lies in inviting and integrating with other cultures. Poorna and Anand very easily adapted to that environment. Knowing that culture, they visited the 'Pasupathinathan Temple' along with their coach Sekhar Babu. The temple was surrounded by dolls, beads and worship supplies. The red flags blew around the saffron-covered temple as a strong wind raged past. The Shiva devotees were waiting in the queue for the Lord's darshan. Other devotees were involved in special worships. After the Lord's darshan, Sekhar Babu purchased some mountaineering gear for Poorna and Anand. Sekhar Babu was able to arrange the Sherpas, Nigma Nuru and Jnanstow. As Poorna and Anand were minors, each of them was assigned two Sherpas. Usually, every mountaineer has only a single Sherpa.

***

Tibet is surrounded by the Himalayas on one side and the Kunlun Mountain ranges on the other side. The beauty of Tibet is reflected in its natural environment. Acclimatization is the process of adapting the bodies to the heights.

The permit papers of the Poorna team were checked by the Chinese and Tibetan governments. All the affairs concerning the permission were taken care of by Sekhar Babu.

The people of Lhasa drank water frequently and added garlic to the water in the bottle to keep their bodies in a hydrating state. Garlic helps to push the oxygen levels to the normal state. As a touristic pleasure, the Poorna team visited the railway station in Lhasa town, and oxygen equipment and masks were available there.

In the process of making the body suitable to existing temperatures while acclimatizing, the body sweats and dehydrates. So, the water intake is the solution. Potatoes were a part of their diet as perfect health demands more carbohydrates.

During their stay in Lhasa, the team spent most of their time in heights greater than their camp, and they trekked to the remote regions. This made sleep difficult for Poorna. After three days of acclimatization, they proceeded on their journey to Gyantse, which was 3950 meters high, on a minibus on the olden highway. Poorna was surprised when she saw the driver handling the steering with his left hands. She asked Sekhar babu and he answered that the steering is usually on the left side in China. This was opposite of India; how to mount the Everest and reach it safely had been the point of discussion in their journey. Everyone on the journey was driven by the strongest desire to climb the Everest. The sky turned black with the passing of time. The headlights of the minibus were unable to display a distance of more than one meter. The driver was cautious and was driving slow.

*Tibetan cat Image Source from Printrest*

As the temperature dropped to minus 10 degrees celsius, the team halted at 'Snowland Hotel'. The journey had tired them out with body pains and headache, and they were waiting for their beds to sleep. When they were getting ready to sleep, an animal resembling a tiger entered the hotel. After observation, it was confirmed to be a scary Tibetan cat. At first, it disturbed Anand's sleep and irritated him, but later it became his good friend.

***

After completing three days of acclimatization in Shigatse, the teamproceeded to Tingri. The bus moved slowly passing through beautiful pastures and valleys. It was a happy journey on the lane road. Every sight was a feast for the eyes through the window. After passing many turning highways and the beautiful valleys in between hills, they reached Tingri. Tingri is a small town situated in the Himalayan mountainranges.

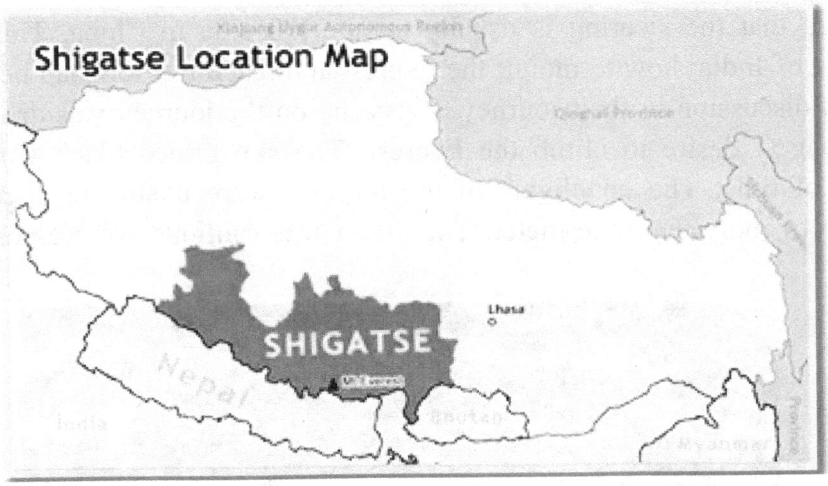


The use of chopsticks to eat food in China interested Poorna. Seeing this, Anand tried eating with chopsticks. The sight of Anand trying to eat noodles with chopsticks and failing amused Poorna. After realizing that they cannot continue with chopsticks, Poorna and Anand resorted to spoons.As Poorna had a small appetite, it became difficult for her to eat foreign noodles. As a game, sometimes she just swallowed them. Many jokes were cracked on this gulping.

Sekhar Babu had taught Poorna about the importance of properly chewing food for mountaineers. He also stressed that these unhealthy habits would make mountaineering difficult. Though Poorna smiled at that instant, she thought of herself as the big problem.

The team visited the Tibetan villages nearby and tried eating their local food. Though Anand easily adjusted to the new food habits, this became difficult for Poorna. To justify herself she made a point about how being an Indian, it was not necessary to adjust to Tibetan food and conditions. Her heart and mind made it difficult for her to adjust to new food. The old habits and patterns disturbed Poorna a bit.

*Source from Sadhanapalli Anand Kumar*

April 14, 2014, the special occasion of Ambedkar Jayanthi arrived. Poorna and Anand wished each other. Praveen Kumar called and wished the children on this occasion. Poorna asked him about her parents' well-being. The conversation with Praveen Kumar made Poorna very happy. After eating two eggs for breakfast at the hotel, Poorna fed the remaining egg to the dog which came to Poorna wagging its tail. She was happy seeing it swallowing the egg.

When Poorna looked at the evening sky, it reminded her of her village, friends, and parents and their discussions. The sparkling stars would relay the message of her firm determination to climb Mount Everest to her parents.

In Pakala, Poorna's parents always thought of her. Poorna's first birthday, first smile, first step, first word – 'father', her resistance while returning from the forest, her escape from the Anganwadi Centre, admitting her in the Tadwai Residential School, and many more memories with Poorna were recounted by Devidas to Lakshmi in a bid to make her happy. Lakshmi hugged Poorna's photo and felt solace.

***

On a daily basis, Sekhar Babu's halted near the Tingri area, understanding the nature of mountain peaks, and reaching their stay by afternoon. The location of the Everest, the way to reach the Everest base camp, and other related information was taught by the coach Sekhar Babu. The Everest base camp was arranged on concrete ground at the 5,200-metre Rongbuk Glacier. Qiantang river flowed beside this camp. Poorna and Anand focused their energies to stay in the ice. They were practicing to adapt themselves to the ice. As a part of this, stood in the ice for some time. They were gathering all of their internal energies to climb Mount Everest.

Poorna understood a part of the trick involved while standing on the rope to reach the peak. Anything that stays with ice for a long time loses its identity, and they were taking all precautions. The Mount Everest mountaineers trained Poorna and Anand with awareness and prepared them for the climb. The strong winds blowing from all directions around them welcomed Poorna and Anand on their adventurous journey.

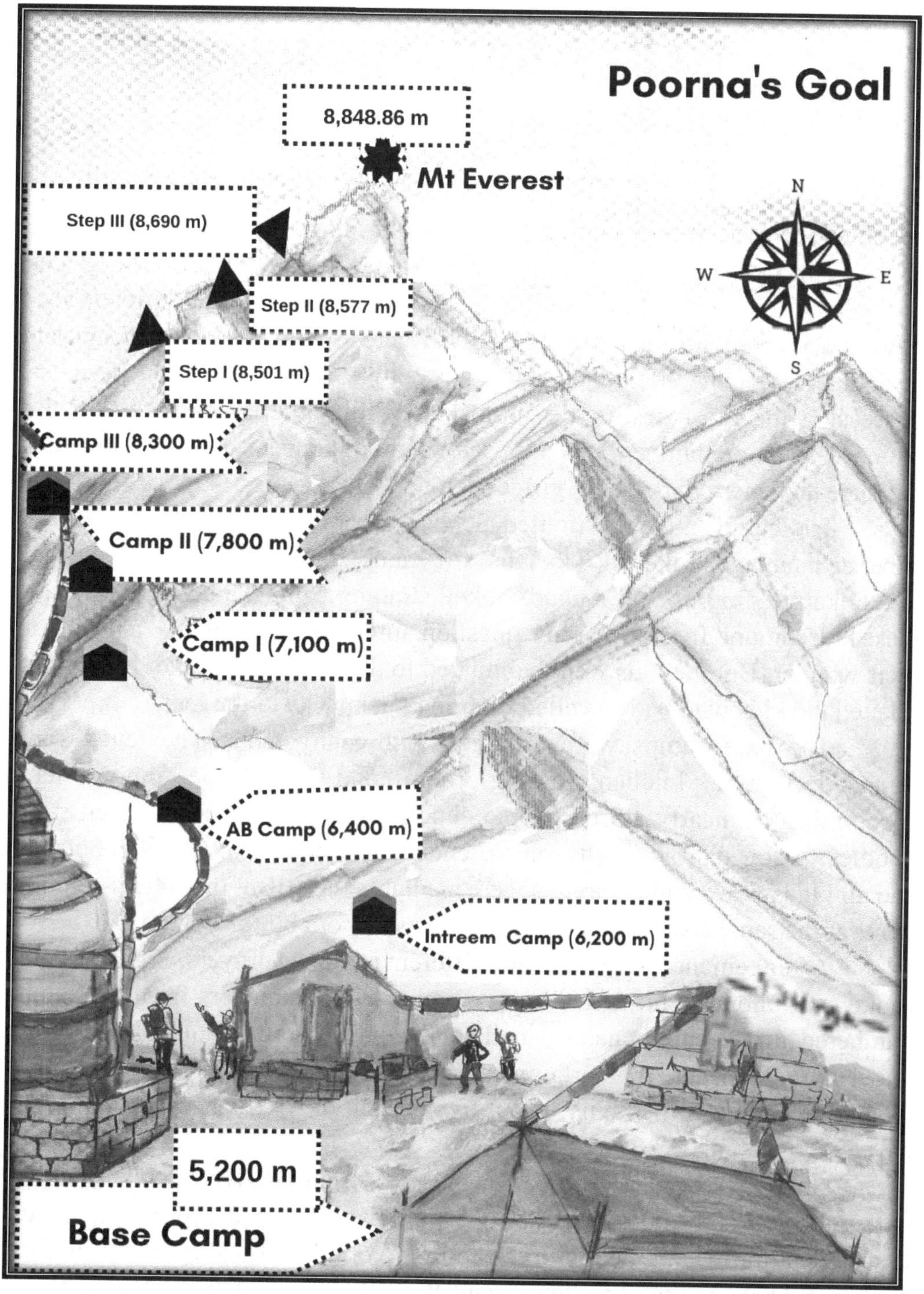
Poorna's Goal
8,848.86 m
Mt Everest
N
W
E
S
Step III (8,690 m)
Step II (8,577 m)
Step I (8,501 m)
Camp III (8,300 m)
Camp II (7,800 m)
Camp I (7,100 m)
AB Camp (6,400 m)
Intreem Camp (6,200 m)
5,200 m
Base Camp

# The Snow Spring

The sage observes everything with a strong will. He becomes the observer separating himself from his pleasures and pains. The Everest in between the hills was appeared like a silent eremite. The obstacles in the atmosphere, the inclined stone faces, and the deficiency of oxygen were the strong weapons of the Everest. Till 2005, the dangerous peak had taken the life of at least one out of five people. The Everest, possessing the most destructive atmosphere, likes the sport of testing the patience of mountaineers. In this sport, mountaineers who invest their patience and energy are easily gifted victory by the Everest.

The camp in-charge invited Sekhar's team to the base camp in the Tibetan language. Like all Tibetans, the camp incharge was reserved and less talkative. Poorna and Anand looked strange to the Tibetans. 'How can these kids mount Everest?' This question might have been the reason for their wonder. But the kids were habituated to those looks. The hot tea served relaxed the kids who had travelled carrying backpacks to the tent.

The base camps were arranged with many tents. The tents were arranged into a kitchen, dining room and hall. The dining tent accommodated nearly thirty people. Food like pizza, burgers, fried rice, noodles, pasta, dal, spaghetti, chips, chocolates, cool drinks, water bottles, and all kinds of tea and cigarettes were available there. But the sellers sold all items at the same cost. Here the price increased from bottom to top.

Arrangements were made for different religious prayers. Some ofthem spoke over phones with their family members. Mountaineers from the camp numbered three, could make a call to the base camp. Though there was television as a means of entertainment, no one seemed interested in it despite its blaring sound. If they only meant to entertain themselves, they would not have come this far.

Sherpas served as helpers in the area. Sherpas live in the Khumbu region, which is 14,000 feet high. As they are born and brought up here, they are naturally equipped with the ability to climb hills. They move swiftly in the cold mountains. The height and the cold changed the make of their

DNA, and they made the hills their living.

Sherpas worship the hills as their deities. Deth Jenlo, a Japanese mountaineer, fell due to High Altitude Cerebral Edema some time ago. That led to the inflammation in his brain, leading to changes in his behaviour, making him hyperactive. He became involved in a quarrel with the Sherpas. He beat one of the Sherpas when he was only trying to help. But the Sherpas, with love, admitted him to the nearby ABC camp. After that, he was shifted to Kathmandu hospital on the plane that arrived from the Lukla and was given treatment. Sherpas were the superhumans who tended to and were loving towards the mountaineers. Frankly speaking, the Sherpas' profession was always dangerous.

Sherpas take up the responsibility of checking the ropes and ladders used while climbing the Everest. They become a part of the will of every Everest mountaineer. Due to this, they climb the Everest many times, a task that seems impossible to most people. Apart from being the guides, they also serve as porters, cooks, and servants. As more people come to climb Mount Everest, Sherpas will be troubled more, but they adjust.

Among 300 dead bodies found around the Himalayan mountains, only 150 had been accounted, and a majority of them were Sherpas. The first man who mounted Mount Everest was an Indian-Nepali Sherpa, Tenzing Norgay, in 1953. He was called Sherpa Tensing. He was also titled 'Tiger of Snow.'

Sherpas are small of moderate complexion, small-eyed, and hard working. The highest valleys surrounding Mount Everest are based in Tibet, and the Sherpas were its tribe. Earlier, they had fought in wars and then migrated as mobile shepherds to the surrounding areas of Tigris.

Sherpas farm by domesticating Yaks. They like Tibetan tea which is made of butter. They belong to the Buddhist division, 'Nyingmapa', and they offer beer to the gods. Their language has a Tibetan dialect, their script is called Tibetan, and they use the Nepali language for their affairs. Tibetans call the Everest 'Chomolungma'.

Sherpas arrange all the things required by the mountaineers on yaks, reach the highest peaks, and make camps for them. As the yaks are trained from a young age to carry heavy weights and climb, on average, a yak climbs the hills with a weight between 68 and 90 kilograms. Yaks walk at the rate of 3 kilometers per hour, and they travel an average distance of 19 kilometers in a day. Yaks play a significant role in transporting mountaineers' food and other things from the base camp to other camps. The yaks act as porters in these mountains by climbing hills in the ice mountains. When the hills are upright, they use a body balancing technique and maintain constant breath while ascending and descending mountains.

*Image Source from National geographic Archives*

Some mountaineers on the mission of climbing the Everest get tired physically and mentally by the time they reach base camp. The practiced manner in which Poorna's team trekked hills and the way they had moulded their bodies at such a young age for the treks surprised the others in the base camp. At this instance, a few whispered that they should mount the Everest while others opposed it. Poorna and Anand were getting habituated to the climate changes. The cold winds blowing at the lowest temperatures sometimes caused headaches in Poorna. This journey felt like the layers of life.

Like water under the mat, the clouds turned black, and night arrived at the tents. The cool winds touched the tents. Poorna disentangled the knots of her tent with her torchlight, opened the curtain, and walked outside. The exterior was body-freezing cold. The dal's smell from the dining hall reminded Poorna of her home. Her mother served the hot food. The family ate together gossiping, creating a warm atmosphere. Thoughts of home deprived Poorna of her sleep.

The ice freezing on the top of the tent appeared like its crown. Seeing this, Poorna imagined herself to be a queen. A small sound alerted her to turn aside and she saw two people coming to her. They were near their thirties and were white-skinned. Poorna thought they might be Europeans. They introduced themselves as Israelis to Poorna, which surprised her. They shared their opinions about Indians. They had thought that Indians only gave importance to education, money, and earnings, and they never expected them to be in sports like trekking. Their view surprised Poorna.

They recounted their experience of the attempt to mount the Nandadevi mountain in India. Poorna felt happy on hearing about Indian mountains in that desolate atmosphere. Both of the Israelis had come to Mount Everest through arrangements made by their government. Anand engaged with them and said that they also came with the government's aid.

***

Sekhar Babu took his team to the Chorten region. That was the area of the Lama Puja. The worships were done on a daily basis there. The history was inscribed in the Pali language on the walls of small rooms inside. In the first room, the lamps were lit using the oil in a big vessel, and prayers were conducted in the blurry light. Lamas wore long coats, and the Buddha statues had a serious look.

A dance performance was conducted there. The dance focused on the old Buddha Puranas, and a few aspects focused on the drama 'Cham.' The yaks carrying the burdens also turned their heads to that music. On witnessing this, Poorna thought about music's impact on birds and animals and made note of their response. Poorna and Anand also participated in the dance.

The Nepali Sherpas sang about 'Sagar Matha' and the Tibetan Sherpas on 'Chomolungma' and prayed. As the audience's applause turned louder, the human form made of flour was burnt, and the celebration ended. This dance celebrates the victory of good over evil.

***

Every morning, Poorna peeped out from her sleeping bag like a confused Australian Kangaroo joey. Every night before sleeping, Poorna looked at the next day's schedule, which comes to her memory in the morning. When Poorna came out to brush, she was welcomed by ten feet of snow. The little shower turned into a snow rain. Nature turned drastically in a very short span of time. The mountaineers who went to the advanced base camp as a part of training came back early due to the unfavorable conditions and rested in the camp the whole day.

Dangers arise due to avalanches if caught in a snow shower. The breakdown of ice and the possibility of avalanches always pose a threat to people. Danger looms over them without any prior indication.

As a part of the expedition, Sherpas officially observe the ropes and ladders on Mount Everest on the season's arrival. They change old ones and replace them with new ones if required. This happens every year. The Sherpas were captured in the avalanches as a part of an expedition in 2014. In the small lane between the Everest and Lhotse Mountain, the ten-building-high snow had fallen as eruption and made the entire region dangerous.

After ten seconds, the captured started shouting and screaming in fear. The one who came out safe shared everything that happened with a radio journalist. He said that he wore an orange helmet, and the situation there was chaotic. The people in the base camp surrounded the radio journalist, The doctor arrived there, made a list of things required for treatment and reported to the Nepali hospital.

The rescue team arrived to enlist the people who took part in the adventurous journey. They made a detailed list of the mountaineers, Sherpas, and Commanders and sent it to the command centre. The camp's Nepalese, Italians, English, Germany, Russian, Japanese, Korean, Hindi and Telugu people-maintained silence, extending their cooperation to the rescue team. The team from the command centre explained the rescue plan on the radio and started collecting the insurance details of the lost lives.

The people captured in the spot of danger had not responded to any change even after hyperventilating them. They were suffering from

Pulmonary Embolism. Some volunteers ran to help them. The person with the orang helmet was trying to signal for a helicopter landing. It was dangerous to land a helicopter there. The counting of humans and everything under the demolition began. Due to the avalanche, 16 Sherpas died, and another eight were missing. Only three lives were saved with great effort in the Kathmandu hospital.

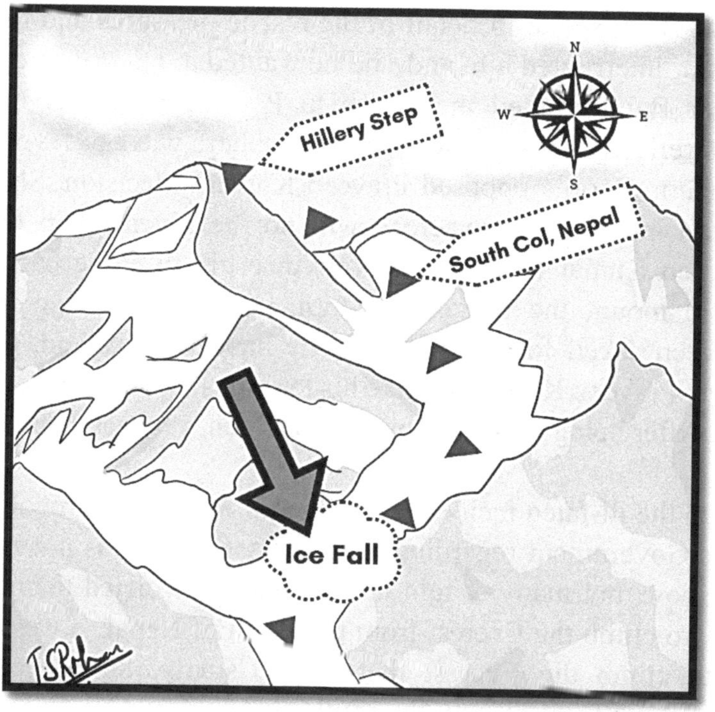


***

On returning from the SWAEROS meeting, Praveen Kumar came to know about the dangerous event that happened near the base camp through the media.The car sped fast to Hyderabad. His thoughts raced faster than the car. The thought of danger to the children made him take the phone into his hands. He had not attended the calls from Sekhar Babu as he was in a meeting. After returning from the meeting, he tried to contact Sekhar Babu but to no use. So, he messaged him regarding the safety of the children.

Under these stressful conditions, Praveen Kumar was lost in his own thoughts. "If anything happens to the children, the change-resistant society will definitely hang me in the cross junction of Panjagutta", he uttered aloud accidentally. The driver handed the water bottle beside him to Praveen

Kumar. The latter emptied the bottle at once.

Praveen Kumar's thoughts were interrupted by a call from his boss, Reymond. Reymond ordered him to get the children back, safe. Praveen Kumar was about to call Shekhar Babu about this, when Sekhar Babu called himself and informed him that the children were safe. He also detailed that the danger occurred in the south, and the children were in the north. While Sekhar Babu spoke in detail of the rescue measures and the process, Praveen Kumar interrupted him and said he wanted to talk to the children.

Sekhar Babu handed the phone to Poorna, who was in the tent. Courage was reflected in her tone. 'The atmosphere was not favourable. So, all of you return. Poorna opposed Praveen Kumar's decision. She also said that the action intended by swaeroes will not be given up in the middle. Though Praveen Kumar tried hard to convince her to come back, she was determined to mount the Everest. In turn, she gave courage to Praveen Kumar. Praveen asked for the phone to be handed to Anand, and Anand supported her. Praveen Kumar felt like his ten rules of success were repeated back to him. After being reassured by Sekhar Babu, Praveen Kumar relaxed.

***

Due to the ill-fated incidents, the Sherpa Association revolted against the Nepalese Government regarding Sherpas' safety. It was not new to lose lives in the snow, but many caught up in the snow worried them. That was the only way to climb the Everest from the south of Nepal. it was closed, no one dared to climb the Everest that way. Usually, 80 per cent of the mountaineers climb Everest from the south.

'Why are we not going from the Nepal side?' Anand questioned Sekhar Babu during trekking practice. "To climb from the Nepal side, there is an age criterion that states that the minimum age requirement is sixteen years. As Poorna is only 13 years old, she has gotten no permission from Nepal. The Tibetan way has no age restrictions, and I had completed my expedition from that side. So, I chose the north Tibetan way", answered Sekhar Babu.

***

The Himalayas are the sign of courage. Poorna's team was trained for two weeks on a daily basis in 'Rongbuk glacier', one of the world'smost dangerous icefalls. As a part of training in the ice falls, they did mockdrills. The ice rocks were sharp-edged here. Behind every step, danger awaits, so being cautious was a must here while walking. Rocks standing there for thousands of years surprise the visitors. These rocks were the embodiment of many pits, unique shapes, and many wonders that surprised the visitors.

Sekhar Babu kept the children busy with training. "The new milestone must always appear as the starting point, and till you complete the expedition, the process must be done with care and confidence." With such words, Sekhar Babu always inspired the children.

"However mighty the Guru might be, he cannot save you at such great heights. Only your practice, the skills learned, self-confidence, and courage can save you. Never let pride get to your head, it will create many difficultiesin the path of success." Sekhar Babu often taught this to children.

Though sleeping bags are comfortable, much time should not be spent in them. More time spent inside the tents also will lead to illness. So, the coach advised Poorna and Anand to spend most of the time outside the tent.

One day Sekhar Babu laughed at Poorna's innocence for feeling that the Everest was quite near. He replied that her thoughts were similar to a fellow under the perception that jaggery tasted salty. Poorna did not understand his words. "Poorna! Do you think the Everest is so near? Do you feel there is nothing else on the path?" He added that this was not a smooth journey on an asphalt road. He also made them understand the dangers involved after eight kilometers and about the deathzone.

Anand questioned him about the death zone. According to studies by the National Geographic Society, the region on top of 7,600 meters was called the death zone. Once the mountaineers reach there, their pulse rate increases, and their oxygen levels drop. If the required oxygen is not supplied, it leads to the malfunctioning of the brain, and in that confusion, they hallucinate, and their thoughts are not clear. Due to indigestion, their appetite decreases, and they will not be interested in eating."Out of the 65 nations that aim at mountaineering every year, only a few of them will make it. A thousand feet away from the goal, obstacles like indigested food resulting in vomiting, sweat from the body turning to ice and eating away the body parts, and the sudden avalanches, can occur all together and take away the life of the mountaineer carrying fear in the backpack. "That region is the 'Death Zone.' Both of you should return safely from that region."

Poorna and Anand fell silent at the words of Sekhar Babu.

From the next day, Poorna and Anand started practising walking on the freezing river with Crampons. Walking with Crampons in the ice burns a thousand calories. A normal walk in the park burns only a fourth of this. The calories spent creates heat in the body. Beads of sweat are formed despite the ice in the surroundings. The turns in the mountainscreate chances of cold winds blowing. The ice axe and Crampons protect against them. Poorna and Anand tried all of them, learned and practiced them with focus, and reached the tent by sunset. The tired schedulemade them sleep.

***

The early sunrays brightened the ice mountains, and the smoke from the ice mountains radiated vapours upward. Poorna, watching nature's beauty, spent thirty minutes practising Surya Namaskars. Was there anyone who would not be astounded by such a breathtaking sight!

The intermediate camp was suitable to start their journey as per the weather reports. After breakfast, at 8 am, Sekhar Babu's team started for the intermediate camp located at a height of 6,100 meters. They reached by six in the evening. Next day, they returned to base camp as well. Along with them, mountaineers from various nations had also reached there. Though Poorna and Anand felt leg pains during this process, they practised well. After practising for two more days, they proceeded to the Advance Base Camp.

There was a tradition of worshipping Sagar Matha for the safety summit of the Everest before the expedition. Before starting for camp after ABC Camp training, the Sherpas told Poorna and Anand about the worship. Following these customs, they attended the worship ritual at Lhama. The trekking weapons, mountaineer gear such as crampons and ice axe etc were piled one above the other by Sherpas.

During this ritual, the Sherpas and Mountaineers pray for their safe journey. Sherpas sing along with Lamas. They offer rice and beer to the deity, Sagar Matha. The flags flying at the towers of the temple wished the best for the mountaineers and children.

An offering was made after the pooja, and many birds came for it. A Lhama sitting on the Stupa, chanting, expressed happiness at the arrival of a bird and said it was the 'Himalayas Python Bird.' A Sherpa said that this bird's arrival was a good omen. After worship, the Lhama pointed towards the stars in the northern sky and asked them to proceed that way. He also handed a signed blessing card to the Sherpas. Poorna meditated for some time in the meditation chamber and concentrated on the Everest. That was only the first step to her mindfulness.

*Source from Sadhanapalli Anand Kumar*

The North Col was situated at a height of 6,400 meters. That day Poorna walked with a new confidence. Overcoming the high-altitude sickness, they climbed a thousand meters at the speed of three kilometres per hour. Poorna was normal, and nothing affected her. Every doctor had checked their medical condition. The ascending and descending of the mountains on a daily basis created trembles and pains in her knees.

It was four days before Poorna's menstrual cycle arrived. She checked for the sanitary pads in her backpack, and relaxed and continued her journey after feeling their presence.

Growth must be planned. Else it risks the lives of mountaineers. The schedule was made so that two days of rest were a part at every camp which was in the path to the Everest. Hastiness was not safe. The eagerness in reaching the goal creates the possibility for conditions like Hypoxia, Pulmonary Edema, and Cerebral Edema. To overcome these conditions, it is necessary to make the body adjust to that atmospheric condition. If that is not done, the ice in the form of force bites would harm the mountaineer.

Without feeling restless, they made daily journeys from the ABC camp to the base camp. Poorna's thoughts were sometimes taken away by the pickled rice her mother fed her. The rotis and boiled green beans had creating a dislike towards food in Poorna. She asked Sekhar Babu an alternative food. After Sekhar Babu's soft reprimands on her food rigidity, Poorna cried, expressing that she could not adjust to such food.

The doctor advised an hour's oxygen intake for Poorna due to vomiting. Poorna was asked to take a rest in ABC Camp. During that time, Anand and Sekhar Babu trekked from ABC to nearby nearby mountains and returned. Poorna was tired physically and mentally. Her tiredness was enveloping her like a whirlpool. Though Poorna did not show up with the symptoms of High-Altitude Pulmonary Edema symptoms, she was feeling tired and restless. As Poorna was feeling uneasy, she returned to base camp from ABC Camp under the doctor's advice.

Poorna felt humiliated when Sekhar Babu consoled her saying that they would wait for her in ABC Camp. The return from ABC Camp to base camp created despair and distress in Poorna. Tears rolled down her cheeks. The lack of a proper diet and vomiting turning into reasons preventing her from making the Everest expedition were silly reasons, she felt. She realized that winning opportunities were nullified by habits. "My tears will not create sympathy or make me reach the summit. I am responsible for my victory. No emotions should affect my journey", Poorna assured herself. While reaching our life goals, sometimes our habits turn up as obstacles. The soldiers frequently participating in the wars were always accommodating to the situations. The adjustment was a compulsion for as long as we lived. Keeping apart other thoughts, Poorna decided to change her diet habits. Rather than flowing against the flow, it was now better to drive in the way of the flow. Poorna gradually changed her food habits.

Poorna focused on prana energy. By imprinting the beauty of the ice-filled mountains in her heart, she experienced great pleasure. Her realization of food habits without resistance made her healthy. After turning healthy, Poorna proceeded to the Advance Base Camp with new confidence.

Nine teams comprising sixty members were waiting for favourable conditions to start the expedition from the ABC Camp. Mountaineers with a strong wish to climb the seven peaks across the seven continents had attended the party conducted by the ABC seven summit club. The experiences shared by the participants in this party surprised Poorna. Among them, a few had climbed the Alphs Mountain Ranges, and they felt happy to climb Mount Everest, in fact it would be the best experience so far. Poorna was glad that she had started her journey with the Himalayas.

Poorna responded with a smile when the group of foreigners enquired about her Everest expedition. At the party, Poorna met Ralf Dujmovits, a German mountaineer who had mounted the 14 peaks of the world. His patience and tolerance were inspiring, and she decided to carry these qualities with her.

As the weather was favourable the following days, they advanced from the ABC camp to the camp-1 (7,100 meters) and stayed there for two days. As per the rules of the Everest expedition, Poorna and Anand would mount the Everest from the camp-1 without a coach and only with the aid of the Sherpas.

They were gradually reach the summit. By the time they reached the camp-2, the doctor had checked Poorna and confirmed that she has no respiratory problems and her heartbeat was normal. But Anand was tired, he felt dizzy, and his soles were numb. Anand was recovering under a doctor's guidance. Sekhar Babu cautioned them to return if any danger arose - life was more important than the expedition. After that, Sekhar Babu returned to base camp.

The wind blowing from higher altitudes were highly dangerous. They reached North Coal Camp-2 safely by using stable ropes, trekking for 7,800 meters. The next day they scaled a height of 8,230 meters and an inclination of ninety degrees and reached Camp-3 in seven hours. Their bodies would have frozen at minus twenty degrees celsius in the tent if not for the protective clothing.

The Sherpa lit the butane gas stove and heated the ice in it. After some time, the ice heated and melted into hot water. He dipped the packaged food in hot water. After two minutes, he served them some boiled jeera-flavoured rice. The food had a different taste since it was only half-boiled. But Poorna kept thoughts of taste away - she felt that nothing was more important than her goal. She gulped down food and ate a few dry fruits and chocolates. Her health so far was good enough for the journey, and no incidents of vomiting and dizziness occurred.

At this altitude, everyone's needs change. The thin line of humaneness between the Sherpas and the mountaineers also slowly vanishes. The Sherpas are looked down upon as people who serve only for money. Many times, thefts of oxygen cylinders happen at such heights. Mountaineers have lost their lives due to these thefts. To save these mountaineers, the Sherpas keep guard over the oxygen cylinders at night.

Poorna and Anand were resting due to tiredness and body pains. They were sleeping in their tents at Camp-3. At five in the evening, Sekhar Babu called the Sherpa on a satellite phone. Sherpa came to Poorna's tent and handed over the phone to her. In her sleepy state, Poorna replied. Sekhar Babu asked her about her safety and intimated that Praveen Kumar had called and as per the weather report, asked them to have dinner and get ready for the summit after nine in the night. Poorna handed the phone over to the Sherpa and took a nap in the meanwhile.

The short nap energized her, and she was now ready for the climb.

***

The first stage of climbing the peak, located at a height of 8,501 meters, takes at least eight hours of time. If the group planned to reach the peak early in the morning, then there would be sufficient time to reach the safe zone by the end of the day. It was highly dangerous to be at such a height without oxygen cylinders after two in the afternoon.

Walking on ice is easy at night. In the mornings, due to the sun's heat, the surface of the ice melts, and the inner surface smoothens. Moreover, if they did not halt at night at Camp-3, oxygen could be saved. If there was a delay, they would need a supply of eight hours of oxygen in the death zone. This was why the night climb to reach by early morning was important.

# Ladders to the sky

It was nine at night on May 24, 2014. Poorna's heart was filled with the desire of victory. Sherpa Nigma Nuru and Jnanstow guided her by displaying the victory signpost. The journey began by checking the headlamp. For Poorna, this was the path to prove her existence. It was a must journey for her and her tribe. She felt this journey was the first step for her to repay her mother's love, and she prayed that it must be victorious.

As Poorna started climbing the mountain amidst the dense ice and brittle hill, her thoughts wandered to her mother. When Poorna asked her what she wanted from Everest, she had cried. Devidas, who was twisting a rope in the verandah, came running to Lakshmi with tears in his eyes, and took her away. Poorna was not sure of what he told her, but after that, Lakshmi smiled happily and hugged her, saying that Poorna would bring home happiness soon.

In the high cold winds of the Himalayas, the sight of Poorna crawling from west to east on the rope would appear to anyone who looked like an effort to embrace the Himalayas. At that time, Poorna and Anand did not have any means to communicate with each other. If everything went smoothly, both of them would meet after the summit.

Straight-edged paths are the most difficult ice paths to navigate, without even a slight inclination. When ascending heights, the oxygen levels in the body drop, and this results in headaches and body pains. Sometimes this may result in unconsciousness as well.

Poorna took her every step with strong determination. The first step for her, the second step for her family, the third step for her tribe's freedom, and the fourth step for women's independence, as she uttered the ten principles of SWAERO and made her journey toward the summit

1. I am not inferior to anyone
2. I shall be the leader wherever I am
3. I shall do what I love and be different
4. I shall always think Big and Aim high
5. I shall be honest, hardworking and punctual
6. I shall never blame others for my failures
7. I shall never beg and cheat
8. I shall repay what I borrow
9. I shall never fear the unknown
10. I shall never give up

R.S Praveen Kumar

*Image Source from Mr K Durga Prasad*

After reaching the 'pyramid stage' of climbing the Everest, dangers arise in three stages in the northern path. The first stage is encountered between a height of 8,501 meters and 8,534 meters (27,890 to 28,000 feet). From here, the path is divided into three ways, and so in every path, a new strategy must be adopted. As the wind's power is immense at this height, it may throw off the mountaineer with such great force that she gets stuck in the brittle ice. The mountaineer must hold on strongly to the rope and cross the zone. There was no time to relax in between.

As Poorna climbed higher, her head started spinning. Though she was a bit dizzy, she plodded ahead. Poorna saw a woman with a jacket coming to her side with determined steps and a smile on her lips. Poorna tried to give her a thumbs-up, but found that her thumb was missing. Poorna realized that she was hallucinating due to the high altitude. The Sherpa reminded her to continue their climb.

Poorna's mind felt intoxicated by the flurry of thoughts. The dizziness increased. She was unable to push her legs forward. The headlights brightened up dark spots, black rocks and ice sparkles, but Poorna felt unable to make any further move. 'I cannot move anymore', she said to herself. On hearing this, the Sherpa reminded her that it was a narrow lane, and it was not possible to rest. With no option but to move, she finally offered a prayer and walked ahead. As soon as she found a place comfortable enough to sit, she sank down with fatigue.

Poorna's face had turned pale because she could not breathe. Immediately, the Sherpa checked the oxygen cylinder and was shocked to find that it was empty. A majority of deaths occur on the Everest due to oxygen deficiency. If anyone fell unconscious midway, there would be no one to take care of them.

The Sherpas were surprised at her ability to walk for such a long time in the absence of oxygen! Sherpa Nigma Nuru immediately changed her oxygen cylinder. Gnanstow, the other Sherpa, was started rubbing Poorna's palm to generate heat and to get her to move. After Poorna was equipped with a new oxygen cylinder, she felt new energy flowing through her, and an experience of wonder for her.

"You have to protect yourself and should never depend on others", Poorna recalled a renowned yoga master, A.R.J. Venugopalacharya's words during training. Poorna took a strong breath, filling her body with more oxygen and relieving it from the fearful state she had experience moments before. After a few minutes of rest, Poorna was restored to normal.

She was able to survive in the oxygen deficiency areas only through the lessons taught by Venugopalacharya. His lessons of focus, hope, and breath control through Yoga served as the master tool for Poorna to keep herself alive. She moved forward with the belief that the teachings of any teacher find their purpose only after they were put into practice at any point of time in life before it was too late. The Sherpas were happy with her renewed energy. Their journey re-started towards the Everest.

Poorna was enraptured by the power of nature which can easily take away anybody's life. The path onwards to the summit was straight. Sometimes during moonlight, the ice sparkled and at other times, black clouds enveloped the moon. The ice in the air tried to reach her head through her eyes, nostrils, and mouth. The changing environment playfully taught the climbers something every moment.

Lifting her goggles, Poorna looked up into the sky. She felt proud of herself for walking in between ice mountains which had turned golden, reflecting the moonlight. The Sherpa observed that Poorna had removed her goggles and shouted. The scream was loud enough to be heard everywhere in the Himalayas. Poorna was advised to put her goggles on again and walk.

At such an altitude, nothing must be seen without goggles and with bare eyes since snowflakes could fall into one's eyes and could be dangerous. Earlier, a Korean mountaineer had lost his eyesight. That was why the Sherpa screamed so hard; after that, the Sherpas encouraged Poorna with their claps when they saw her focus on climbing.

Crossing each peak before the Everest felt like a sign of victory to Poorna. A half-hour journey would reach a height of 8,534 meters. Even at such great heights, her lungs were able to draw in oxygen from the cylinder. It was Poorna's practice that helped her tolerate strong cold winds without getting affected by high altitude sickness. All this was possible only because of her practice.

The Sherpas observed Poorna carefully. They were glad to note that she did not have any troubles because of the high altitude. They welcomed her to the second stage after rechecking her oxygen cylinder. The second stage lies in the ascension range of 8,577 meters to 8,626 meters (28,140 feet). In this stage, the journey turns a bit difficult and complicated. The Sherpas suggested that Poorna wear the crampon in this stage. Poorna got to use the equipment she purchased in Nepal.

*Image Source from Pinterest*

Aluminium ladders were used to cross the brittles in between crevasse. Walking on the ladder was highly dangerous. The crampons added to the difficulty in crossing the ladder.That was a terrible experience. The mountaineer must focus on the ladder and not on the valley. Sometimes the ladders were ten feet far, and at other times they were 45 feet far. Ropes are used to cross them carefully.The tired climbers needed to relax. They rested till the ice cleared. From where they rested, all the camps were visible. To overcome Acute Mountain Sickness (AMS), the body must be hydrated. The water improves the functioning of red blood cells in the body. Dehydration then leads to fatigue, nausea, and headaches that weaken the body. Poorna tried to open the water bottle. As the hand gloves would not let her open the water bottle, she removed them, opened the bottle, drank water, and placed it in the backpack. She checked her fingers and toes. After confirming that all was well, she put her gloves back on. "I am in the Himalayas, and I must observe everything in motion", she said to herself.

*Image Source from Pinterest*

The trekking path was a narrow lane, enough only for a single person to walk. The oxygen mask was a must even while talking. Climbing the Everest in such situations would bring her victory, changing her and her society. This was the belief she had grown up with since her childhood. Despite feeling weak and dizzy many times, she walked with determination towards the peak. The Himalayas creates not only awe but also another feeling which is inexpressible. Early in the morning, the sky shone with stars. Poorna felt like climbing and grabbing a few stars from it.

The mountaineers had reached the final stage, and at this stage, the altitude was in the range of 8,690 to 8,800 meters (28,510 to 28,870 feet). At fifty degrees incline in the pyramid-shaped peak, Poorna clipped and unclipped the screw of rope and crawled forward. During trekking practice, the Everest appears close, but that was not true. Reaching the Everest was like reaching an oasis in the desert.

In the narrow lane, the ladder extended up to thirty feet. Though there was a signpost indicating that the mountaineers going through the north way must take a left turn, the Sherpas indicated to the left again with their hands to make this clearer. Because there was no signpost earlier, a mountaineer had fallen down the valley. From then, the signpost was kept there. From there, the summit of the Everest summit was just 200 meters away.

Nobu Kazu, the Japanese mountaineer, could not climb the Everest successfully despite four attempts. During the fifth attempt, in the third stage, he was caught in the narrow valleys due to the strong winds and was there for two days. Surrounded by ice, it lead to frostbite. He lost both hands in this attempt, and his dream of summiting Everest could not become a reality.

Poorna, with a gradient varying from thirty to seventy-five degrees, reached climbed over the rocks to reach the peak. To cross the pyramid-shaped peak, she stuck like a lizard to the wall and crawled over safely. She was just a foot away from the summit. She asked for her location every two minutes. With patience, the Sherpa was answering that she was almost near.

Ushering in sunrise, the ice-covered mountains shone like gold on the eastern side, and the dark black dissolved in the white ice. It wasearly in the morning, and the way was a little visible. Valleys surrounded the path, and the oxygen tank on her back was displaying more than it originally was.

Poorna stopped suddenly. Ahead of her, a corpse hung from an old rope. The corpse wore mountaineering gear, an oxygen tank, and crampons. One hand of the corpse had a ice axe. Poorna's heart raced at the sight, and her legs started trembling. It took her a few seconds to control herself. The mountaineers' breath evaporated in front of the power of the Everest. He might have come this far with the desire of victory. All his desired were now numbed.

The Sherpa approached Poorna. He opened a water bottle and made her drink water. He consoled her with his signs and urged her to move forward. "I will be grateful to the Sherpas forever. Could I have reached my goal without their efforts?" Poorna was moved by their services. Taking in a strong breath of oxygen, she reached the peak, filling her body with renewed energy.

The study of the history of the Everest makes clear the wheres and hows of a journey. During the climb, many secrets of survival can be learned. 'I can do anything' is the most important principle in life. Risking life to some extent also adds excitement. This area becomes a laboratory for studying the human anatomy at greater altitudes. The functioning of the brain under heavy ice and winds can be studied here. The guide to universal knowledge lies here. This cannot be considered a tourist spot. Poorna observed her journey of scaling every height andthe process of reaching the summit with her heart and soul. She experienced her heart struggling here for survival.

*Image Source from Pinterest*

Junko Tabei, the woman Japanese mountaineer, wrote the following in the American Online Journal, 'The Seven Summits.' When she with her team was in the Everest expedition, her teammates were buried in ice at the height of 7,000 meters. By the time the Sherpas dug and dragged Tabei out of the ice, she was unconscious. Her friends lost their lives. Tabei recovered slowly with treatment. She started her Everest expedition again and set the record of the first woman mountaineer to climb the Everest. "Never give up on your journey, and your hope" were her inspiring words of success.

From the time of our ancestors, all of us have been mobile beings; when our lives stopped being stationery, humans lost their humanity in the process. Poorna could hear the sound of her own breath while taking in oxygen from the cylinder. She moved forward. The courage in a woman is natural and it had driven Poorna's journey.

The innocence of childhood reached the universal love-spreading summit. At a temperature of minus 35 degrees celsius, the peak resembled the shape of a dining table. Poorna looked around in silence. From there, the paths and camps she had crossed were visible. This was the most memorable experience of her life. She felt that the scene she beholded in front of her was Lord's nature, a symbol of beauty The Sherpa's smile was a witness to all her feelings and experiences.

Poorna, in search of her dreams, came to the call of Everest. She felt it was the greatest tribute to the great humans who thought of humanity as the purpose of life. Malavath Poorna's climbing Everest was a gesture to prove that she was the heir to the most incredible human Dr. B.R. Ambedkar. To be an existing example of all these, she mounted the top of Everest as a part of SWAERO.

A Sherpa sitting on a black rock looked at Poorna. The other Sherpa took out a t-shirt from the backpack. "The youngest girl to climb the Everest", was printed on the shirt, and he waited for Poorna to wear it. Nigma Nuru and Gyanstow made a thumbs up and shared their happiness. She stored her memories in the camera she brought.

She remembered all the people who inspired her from the beginning. She displayed the flags that were bought along. She hoisted the Indian flag. She hoisted the flags displaying Ambedkar, who fought against discrimination and S.R. Shankaran, who dedicated his life to the poor. At last, the SWAERO flag was hoisted with pride for the great thoughts it upheld. Poorna was highly excited. Her heart was filled with happiness. Her eyes turned wet when she was reminded of the long-time poojas performed by her parents for this moment. She thanked her coaches, Sekhar Babu and Parmesh Singh, on this occasion. She felt proud of this moment as it was her chance to show her gratitude towards Praveen Kumar, who was the designer, planner and implementer of this mission. She thanked everyone who was responsible for her victory.

A small stone on Everest can narrate the whole experience into a beautiful story. Poorna asked the Sherpas for two stones. The Sherpa collected two stones buried in the ice and gave them to her. She considered one among them a memory of her school and the other a memory of her summit and happily stored them in her bag.

*Image Source from Sadhanapalli Anand Kumar*

This victory was the symbol of Poorna's patience, perseverance, and sensitive focus on the climb at the young age of thirteen. The highest peak of the world, which had challenged many, was challenged and won over by a thirteen-year-old girl with her foot on it, because of her perseverance. The sun rays being the witness, Poorna had set the record as the "Youngest girl to climb the Everest".

After reaching the base camp from the summit, mountaineers from the Chinese Mountaineering Federation congratulated her. They took photos with her. After the path was cleared in 2014, Poorna had been the first person to mount the Everest. An hour after Poorna, Anand also mounted

Everest. The Nepali radio announced that Poorna and Anand were victors, and they had mounted the Everest and Poorna had set the record for Summit the peak at an early age.

*Image Source from Printrest*

After her victory at the Everest, Poorna visited the Pashupatinath temple in Kathmandu, Nepal. There the stores were run by women. Prayer wheels of different shapes, flutes, bells, Buddha idols, statues, beads, silver bells sounding music, children's toys and many others were sold in the stores. Poorna purchased a chain of beads for her mother, and ornaments like earrings, necklaces and finger rings for her friends.

Poorna's face was dark-complexioned, resembling chocolate. As both of her eyes turned red, she checked with a Nepali hospital and returned to India.

After reaching India, she shared her experience of victory with Narendra Modi, the Prime Minister and Pranab Mukherjee, the President at that time.

By the time she reached the Hyderabad airport, her mother was waiting for her. Her mother brought something in a box, and the sight of the box made her salivate. Poorna's mother served her food with her hands, and it tasted wonderful to her.

As the barren lands turn to fertile with rains, the nutrient-rich food in her stomach made her feel alive. After 52 days, she had consumed food with satisfaction.

Poorna's victory got middle-class families to turn their heads towards social welfare residential schools. Poorna won many national and international honours. She also acted as representative of the United Nations Organisation from Telangana state.

*Image Source from IndiGo Archives*

As a symbol of women's power, the letters 'POORNA' were imprinted on India's Indigo Airways. Poorna was an inspiration for many downtrodden sections to take a step forward toward education.

# My Journey to Everest in Mind

Our generation, armed with IT skills, frequently travels abroad, and has always needed to prove itself and continuously work for a livelihood. The abundance of humility, attention, patience, skills, time, and cooperation do not make up for the lack of a literary environment, an impediment to inculcating the habit of writing. Brought up in a working-class family, writing was a mighty task for us.

Writing is not a simple task. While writing, thought get stuck sometimes, and the right words and expressions vanish. Letters disappear from words when looked at with care and caution. And at other times, thoughts themselves vanish when wracking our brains to focus. As the saying goes, beautiful flowers are for God, and so is the unwritten book, in response to 'for whom?'.

Conventionally aspirational labels like that of a doctor, actor, engineer, and corporate employee have stuck to us like a disease. More and more time spent in life's comfort zones are driving us to the point of irritation.

Existence is such that it forces us to repeat things done yesterday, today as well. Changing oneself is like a sharp-edged knife. Change is not easy for anyone. Progress requires us to expand our horizons and inculcate the scientific temper to study and research. New thoughts and new habits can strengthen life.

Only people truly determined to do so will have the desire to change themselves. If you spent an hour every day on social studies, you will gradually understand social structure. Similarly, creativity imbues itself if you write daily, making you a writer. By changing personal identity, the personal development is accelerated. Newly acquired traits become part of the personality with practice. This later helped you work the way you want.

Devidas, Poorna's father, helped me with information required for this book for which I thank him whole-heartedly. The study of social sciences, neuroscience,philosophy, and history were required to write this book. Along with extensive notes made from these books to help with my writing, I also engaged myself in a daily walk, and in a way, this book is a fruit of my lonely strolls, Thoughts at night would turn into a typed-out story that was refined during the evenings. This way, I was engaged in the process the whole day, and the journey of writing 'Everest in Mind' proceeded with gusto.

Malavath Poorna's goal is larger than life, and it is different, unique, and strange as well. Poorna's steps reflect unabandoned hope, confidence, hard work, service, and a fighting spirit against failure. Poorna grew beyond her age and distinguished herself from the category of age. She always welcomed change. She reached the peak through the changes she made in herself. 'Everest in Mind' is the compass needle for those who break the old traditions and work for a better chance.

Intending to mount the world's seven highest peaks, Poorna steams ahead. Till now, she has scaled seven mountains.

Success is calculated by most people on the measure of steps, kilograms and university degrees. However, success must be decided by the measure of the depth of thoughts a person has. Inspiration becomes a factor more important than only comforts and capabilities, when one sets out to achieve a goal. Inspiration itself is nothing but a part of human personalitywhich speedens up the capacity to reach goals and yield the best results.

The characters in this book have the same personality. I have observed three main traits in them. First, an activeness in responding. Second, people who understood self-importance. Third, they are people with the spirit of service.

Wg Cdr T. Sridharan, Retired IAF Officer, vastly experienced in Mountaineering, Skiing, White Water Rafting, for more than 35 years. Climbed many peaks and led many mountaineering expeditions. Still active in trekking to various parts of Himalayas.

He played a crucial role in training and preparing Poorna and Anand for the Mt.Everest expedition during winter training in Ladakh. He still gives his valuable time and mentors Transcend adventures in every major expedition. He is also a life member of the Indian Mountaineering Foundation New Delhi and also a member of the Many Governing Council (Executive body) of IMF for 20 years.

Surekha Banavath stood as the first escort to the children in their Tiger Hill journey. As a national wrestler, she understood the children's psychology and the time spent with her made the children feel pleasant always. She made the snacks for the children and brought them in two tins.

Surekha can be considered the mother in the form of a teacher for the children. Surekha's role was very pivotal in the victory journey of the children. She always stressed that the girls were equally capable of mountaineering sport and encouraged them. Surekha bought sanitary napkins for the girls who were in the mountaineering sport of Tiger Hills, which indicates her motherly instinct for the children. The children became very close to Surekha due to her mother nature.

She turned up early in the training and reflected the spirit of inspiration in the children. The sad demise of Surekha, while she was pregnant, due to illness in 2015 was unfortunate and sorrowful.

Thoughts propelling human intelligence are the driving forces for success. Even a small thought can be realised to a great extent. I reveal a secret here. Nobody thinks of the other's progress. A person's growth or decline in a field is decided by their dedication to the work.

Rallabandi Srilatha, the national handball sportswoman. She was the second escort for the children for a span of nearly eight months. She fed nutritious food to children as per the timings given by the coach Paramesh. To encourage children and to develop the victory spirit in them, she practised running at 4 am in the early morning. She also ascended the Ladakh summit as a helper to Poorna. Her patience surprised the other trainees of Ladakh. Every night she slept only after Poorna and Anand were a sleep.

Rallabandi Srilatha

In the Gurukul School R.S. Praveen Kumar made many changes at the micro-level. The congregation of changes turned into a great success. The studies of children improved. The results are so fast that the external society is unable to track them. Taking up the responsibility for thoughts plays an important role here. Praveen Kumar, who was determined to changethe community, maintained balance. As he took the responsibility of reforming society, he developed insights into the effects of his changes in reality. Praveen Kumar did everything whole heartedly.

Thinking, preparation and strategy are essential for any victory. To achieve a goal, proper planning and acute awareness are required. Memory is raw material for thoughts. Sekhar Babu's planning has been vital to Poorna's success.

One hopes that readers of her inspiring story will be inspired for a great change, and that they will have the perseverance to succeed.

Reading this book is a proof of your will. That aiming for high goals in life makes a person happy is 'Everest in Mind's logline.

Sometimes our efforts do not succeed, leading to disappointment. The cooperation of several people, directly or indirectly, were involved inthe completion of this book.

I visited Rajasthan from Malaysia to gather Banjara traditions collection. In 'Jaipur Literature Festival', I am able to get the required books.

These rare books and the experience of spending time in ice mountains helped me write this book. I visited the Kedarnath mountain range for trekking practice to experience the sights, environment, traditions, and culture with my family.

*Kaushik Reddy Pamireddy and Tejo Samiksha Pamireddy (Left to Right)*

This is 3,583 meters (11,755 feet) above sea level near the Chorabari lake. This experience made us understand how dangerous trekking is here.

During this journey, my daughter Tejo Samiksha (8 years), and my son Kaushik Reddy Pamireddy (12 years) hoisted their school (Regent International School, Malaysia) flag and felt very happy. During this writing journey, my wife Smt. Padmaja extended her full support and became part of the book as a co-writer. She designed the cover page of the book and proofread it. My special thanks to her.

Author's family at Kedarnath

*Kaushik Reddy and Tejo Samiksha hoisted their Regent International school flag*

# The End

At Regent International Schools we nurture our students with virtues and strive towards making them global citizens. There is no limitations or boundaries on how one can become a global citizen with the values of diligence, confidence, compassion or perseverance. Malavath Poorna is one such example.

'Poorna,' when translated from Sanskrit denotes 'fulness,' or 'fulfilled.' And it is the same feeling that will pervade your heart when you read her story - *Everest in Mind.* Her determination, perseverance, courage, along with her humble beginnings sets an example of what the humankind can achieve.

*Everest in Mind* encompasses all rhetoric and quite aptly put, tells you the story of the tribal girl, Malavath Poorna who was raised in nature at the Pakala Village in Telangana. Where reaching the most nearby shop required a five-kilometre walk, the abundance of the forests and animals were vicinal. The humble beginnings, the stories from her father, and mother nature created 'Poorna,' the miraculous. It shows you the world without technology, or the hustle and bustle, and teaches you that you can be a winner, and fill your heart with a sense of achievement.

The narration which includes Indian history, social and cultural disparities prevalent in the country along with the achievements of a young girl will provide inspiration to millions in the days to come. May Poorna's determination, courage, passion, resilience inspires the future generation.

Regent International Schools wishes Poorna all the best for all future expeditions.

Regent International Schools,
Malaysia

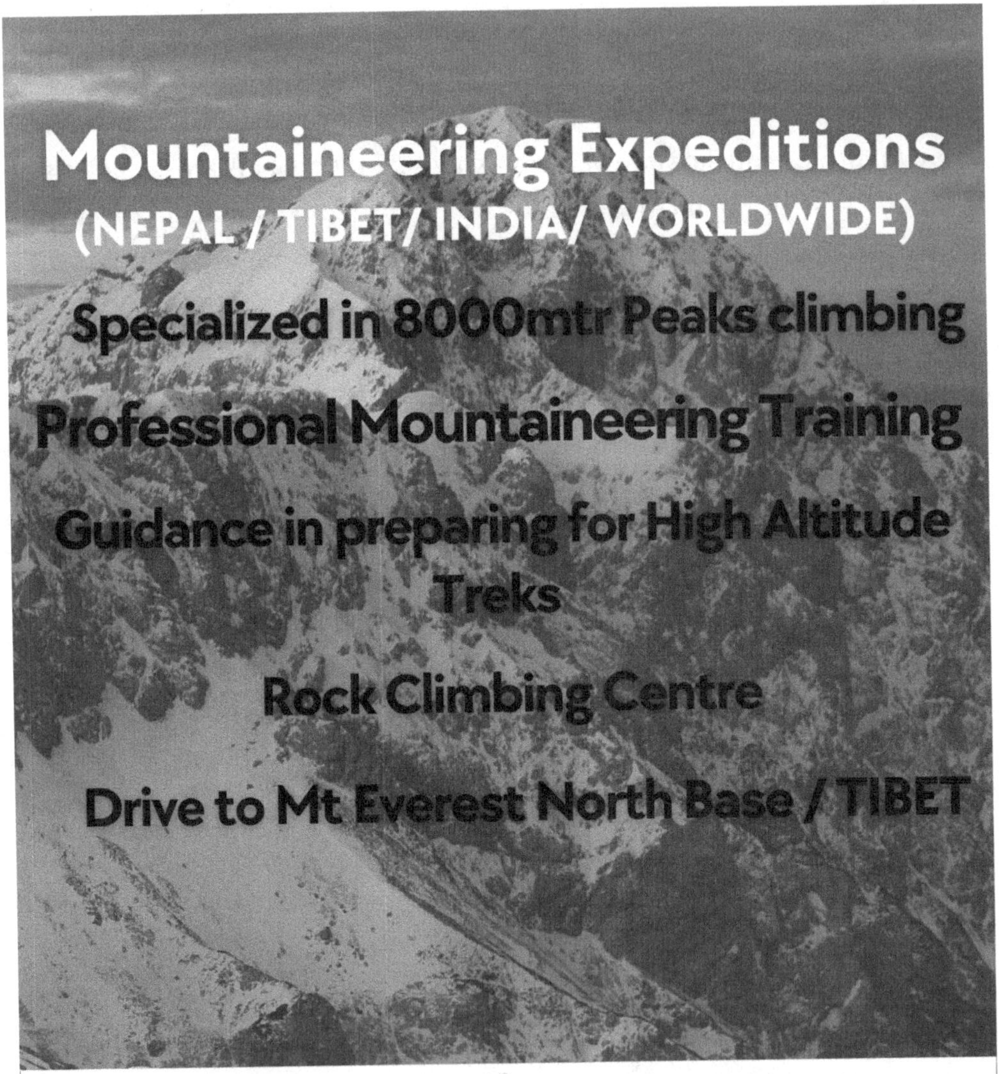
Mountaineering Expeditions
(NEPAL / TIBET/ INDIA/ WORLDWIDE)
Specialized in 8000mtr Peaks climbing
Professional Mountaineering Training
Guidance in preparing for High Altitude Treks
Rock Climbing Centre
Drive to Mt Everest North Base / TIBET

9 788195 677320

Printed at Repro India Ltd.